The Organizational
Politics of
Criminal Justice

The Organizational Politics of Criminal Justice

Policy in Context

Virginia Gray
University of Minnesota

Bruce Williams
The Pennsylvania State University

LexingtonBooks
D.C. Heath and Company
Lexington, Massachusetts
Toronto

Library of Congress Cataloging in Publication Data

Gray, Virginia.
    The organizational politics of criminal justice.

    Includes index.
    1. Criminal justice, Administration of—United States. I. Williams,
Bruce, joint author. II. Title.
HV9304.G69   364'973   77-18590
ISBN 0–669–02108–3

Published simultaneously in Canada

Printed in the United States of America

International Standard Book Number: 0–669–02108–3

Library of Congress Catalog Card Number: 77–18590

To Lynn and Mel

Contents

List of Figures
and Tables

Figures

Tables

Preface and Acknowledgments

This book examines the attempts of a federal agency—the Law Enforcement Assistance Administration (LEAA)—to alter the policies pursued by criminal-justice agencies at the state and local level. LEAA is an agency with few friends and admirers in the halls of Congress or the offices of the executive branch. It is widely viewed as a failure, and at this writing (spring of 1980), the agency, facing either total elimination or a severe reduction in funding, seems likely to become a casualty of the budget-balancing fever sweeping American government. Whether or not LEAA survives, however, much can be learned from its experiment in using block grants to achieve federally set goals. The experiment was in large part a failure—and may be symptomatic of the broader failure of the federal block-grant concept.

We suggest that the dynamics of federal influence in state and local policymaking are best understood in terms of interorganizational relations. The success or failure of federal policymaking is best understood in terms of interorganizational relations. The success or failure of federal policymaking organizations is determined by the degree to which they can successfully manipulate the environments of state and local agencies and thereby alter their policy outputs. The burgeoning theoretical literature in the sociology of organizational behavior illuminates the ways in which organizations, or systems of organizations, respond to changes in their environments. We apply this literature to LEAA's administration of the criminal-justice block-grant program.

The conclusions drawn from this application of organizational theory are timely, whether or not LEAA successfully "dodges the bullet" of federal budget-cutters. These conclusions are particularly relevant during a period of fiscal crisis and budgetary austerity. They indicate that federal spending has not achieved federal goals. Moreover, such spending is unlikely to achieve these goals except under two conditions: a drastic increase in the amount of spending (an extremely unlikely prospect), or a change in the overall strategy pursued by the federal government.

In brief, we argue in this book that the use of federal block-grant funds as a means of altering state and local policies is not likely to be effective unless the amounts are significantly increased or their administration is altered. Further, federal goals may not be best served through the allocation of federal monies as the carrot and their withdrawal as the stick. Our findings suggest the necessity of reconsidering the present system of federal grants to states and localities. As the grants are presently administered, they are unlikely to achieve federal policy goals.

Our findings suggest the superior efficiency of an alternative strategy to the use of the block grant: the creation of a set of shared values between policy-makers at different levels of government through, for example, increased professionalism. The carrot-and-stick approach to securing coordination in a federal system (what we call a power-dependence strategy) has not been markedly successful; the alternative tactic of increasing the shared values within the federal system (what we call an exchange strategy) has worked better. We find that, where LEAA has succeeded, it has been because of a reliance upon the latter and not the former.

The approach that we develop for analyzing policymaking in a federal system is generally applicable to other areas of public policy. It should be relevant to students of public policy as well as practitioners. Our empirical findings, although dealing only with LEAA, have broader implications for the design and administration of federal grants and the rational evaluation of the goals that those grants can be expected to achieve.

This book could not have been completed without the aid of a number of individuals and institutions. Bruce Williams is indebted to the Department of Political Science, the Computer Center, and especially the Liberal Arts Data Lab at The Pennsylvania State University for logistical support. Virginia Gray is indebted to Robert Crew, whose agency provided her with an initial learning experience in criminal justice; Betsey Reveal for an insider's perspective; Michael Mulkey, who provided access to data; the Brookings Institution's Guest Scholar Program; the Graduate School and the Department of Political Science, University of Minnesota, for financial and logistical support; the graduate students in her seminars for patiently listening to these ideas over the years; Julie Murphy for expert typing; Mel Gray for his supportive role; and Brian Gray, who thought the book should be much shorter. Finally, both authors are forever in the debt of Lynn Appleton for her merciless and endless critiques of our writing. Our attitudes about "final" drafts will never be the same.

1 Public Policy in a Federal System

The widespread recognition that advanced industrialized societies may be ungovernable has prompted a new concern with federal governments' control in decentralized systems. Governments are faced with complex problems whose solutions require the coordinated action of a number of independent actors dispersed throughout different levels of government and society. In this book one such complex and seemingly intractable problem—crime—is examined. The rate of crime is not particularly responsive to direct government action, at least in democratic societies. Crime is a function of demographic characteristics of the population, such as the size of the youth population and tne level of unemployment. In the United States the crime-control problem is further complicated by the fact that the national government possesses little police power but must rely on state and local governments to fight most crime. Crime control, therefore, provides a good arena in which to observe a federal government's attempts to direct the activities of its constituent governments in solving a difficult problem.

Conventional wisdom (embodied in sayings such as "he who pays the piper calls the tune") would lead us to expect that federal attempts to direct a decentralized system ought to be increasingly successful. In the past, states and localities raised and spent large sums of money at their own discretion. Today federal aid is the largest single source of revenue for state and local governments combined.[1] Thus, the federal agencies ought to be better able to call the tune than in the past. Yet observations indicate that policy outcomes are not noticeably better now that services are more centrally funded (though still locally delivered). The inability of governments to solve such public problems is due as much to changes in relations among organizations as it is to the complexity of the problems. The context within which governments operate has changed: the environment has grown more organizationally dense.[2] This book documents the effect of organizational context on federal-state relations in criminal justice in the United States.

In the United States the federal government's response to its failures in intergovernmental problem solving has been to experiment with a variety of different fiscal mechanisms: the categorical grant, general and special revenue sharing, and the block grant. The latter two mechanisms increase the control of state and local decision makers over the use of federal funds in comparison with their control over categorical funds. In the criminal-justice area, the federal government has chosen the block-grant mechanism for supplying funds to state and local governments. The premise is that crime is a national problem that can

1

be solved best by central funding and coordination of state and local efforts in fighting crime. The state decision makers, being better informed about their particular crime situation than the federal officers, can more wisely allocate the money to a series of projects designed to stop crime. This book explores how states allocate this type of "free" money in the criminal-justice area.

The states' allocation of free money offers an interesting contrast to how states (and cities) allocate their own revenues. Past studies of the policy process at the state or local level focused on how states and cities allocate revenues raised from their own sources. Research showed that the wealth of a governmental unit fundamentally structures the amount of services offered to its citizens, that is, rich states offer diverse and high quality programs while poor states offer very little because they cannot afford to deliver the services.[3] Politics does not determine the type and level of programs citizens enjoy, as political scientists originally expected. For state programs funded by federal aid (such as criminal justice), the economic constraints on the policy process are constant across states. State characteristics (such as political factors) structuring the funds' allocation can be analyzed, without the overriding effect of economics.

The substantive focus is on an intergovernmental policy funded at the national level and implemented at the state level. This kind of intergovernmental relationship permits the study of the politics of federal control in an organizationally dense system. The free-money aspect permits the study of political effects without the confounding effect of economics.

Conceptual Difficulties in the Study of Policy and Politics

Policy is a course of action followed by a set of actors in dealing with a problem. A *public policy* is a sanctioned course of action pursued by governmental authorities for the purpose of achieving a governmental end. Policy is a concept, as Heclo says, larger than a decision and smaller than a social movement.[4] In this study a series of decisions in which state planning agencies allocate federal funds to other criminal justice agencies is examined. These authoritative decisions are aggregated into courses of action, which are directed toward several governmental goals (innovation, coordination, and so forth). The allocation of funds to projects constitutes a policy toward crime.

Since public policies are produced by governments and are the goals of political action, it follows that political scientists should consider the relationship of political behavior to public policy. Yet for the most part, our studies indicate that political action does not alter public policy. The failure of political scientists to establish this linkage stems from a narrow definition of politics. Nearly everyone embraces the Eastonian definition of politics as the authoritative allocation of values. Indeed, most comparative state-policy scholars use Eastonian systems theory to guide their research. In practice, however, most policy researchers define politics as electoral politics or, more narrowly, as interparty competition. The broadest definition of political action usually includes a narrow range of political factors such as interest groups, citizen participation, and legislative apportionment. Bureaucrats are rarely included as political actors. When administrators have been included, however, researchers have found them to have more important roles in the policy process than the traditional political actors.[5]

Most comparative-policy studies (whether local, state, or cross-national) implicitly assume that politics is separate from administration—an assumption that has been repeatedly challenged in other quarters since the late 1940s.[6] Given the importance of the bureaucracy, our understanding of the policy process is not likely to improve through further studies of the inputs of citizens or of the conversion processes of legislatures: the administration of policy must be examined.

Traditional approaches' second conceptual flaw is their implicit definition of policy as either an output or an outcome. *Policy outputs* are legislative acts; *policy outcomes* are the long-term consequences of legislative acts. Comparative studies typically omit the *implementation stage,* in which bureaucrats carry out the policy directive. Case studies of the implementation stage show that the relationship between legislative intent and bureaucratic action varies dramatically and affects the policy outcome.[7]

One reason, of course, for the omission of implementation from the definition of policy is the omission of bureaucrats from the category of political actors. Broader definitions of policy and politics in studies would contribute to a fuller understanding of how governmental action affects policy. Such an understanding is particularly important in the present era when many policies are enacted nationally but implemented locally. Similarly, implementation is an important phase for revenue sharing and block grants. These are the fiscal mechanisms for nation-state relationships whereby subnational governments allocate the funds as well as deliver the service.

Traditional approaches' third conceptual failure in the study of politics and policy is their focus on the isolated political actor rather than on the interaction of actors. Studies of mass political behavior generally consider the individual voter making an individual calculation about how to vote. To some extent this individualist perspective is due to the current dominance of economic rather than sociological theories. The reliance on national sample survey data reinforces this individualistic perspective. However, some theorists are increasingly aware of the fact that political behavior, like other social behavior, occurs in a context. A growing number of scholars is beginning to incorporate information about context (for example, neighborhood) with information about the individual in order to predict behavior.[8]

As do most studies of mass political behavior, comparative state studies of public policy typically ignore the context within which systemic factors operate to produce policies. The influence of systems theory produced this situation.[9] At least at the state level, the limited number of governmental units available for statistical testing has maintained it. Typically, independent variables are modeled as additive in their effects, implicitly assuming that the effect of political variables on policy is invariant regardless of the type of policy, need for the policy, level of resources, or actions of other governments. Although a few scholars of public policy have called for interactive models of the policy process,[10] Downs is the only scholar who has attempted to study contingent effects.[11]

The Perspective of Interorganizational Theory

Public policies are increasingly determined by the interactions of large public and private organizations. The impact of one type of organization—the interest group—has been observed in Latin American and Scandinavian countries' corporatist policy process, as well as in American policy areas where structural interests prevail (for example, health).[12] For a decade, scholars have noted that U.S. intergovernmental relations are dominated by the interactions of local, state, and federal bureaucrats operating within functionally specific areas.[13] This observation suggests that another type of organization—the professional association—might have an important influence in the policy process.

Given the focus on the interactions of organizations, neither the systems approach at the macro level nor the decision-making approach at the micro level is appropriate. The unit of analysis is the agency, a public organization; the appropriate behavior to be analyzed is the interaction of the agency and other actors, including other organizations. A theory cast at this level, between the system and the individual, is likely to explain differences in public policies.

The most fertile source of organizational theory is the field of sociology. In the last decade, several political scientists have used organizational theory, largely borrowed from sociology, to explain a variety of political phenomena.[14] However, these explanations focus almost exclusively on the effect of intra-organizational factors on political decision making. It is important to move beyond this focus and examine the relationships among organizations, between organizations and their context, and the effect of these relationships on politics and policy.

In the past decade, sociologists have moved toward an interorganizational perspective on the study of complex organizations. In organizational sociology it is widely accepted that an organization's behavior and structure are largely contingent on characteristics of its environment.[15] Interorganizational theory examines the consequences of an important development: society's increasing organizational density. As density increases, an organization's environment increasingly consists of fields (or networks) of other organizations.[16]

This characterization is applied to explain *picket-fence federalism:* the relevant environment of a state government is other agencies at all governmental levels. Rather than generalists, such as elected officials, functional specialists dominate state governments. When applied to intergovernmental policy, the sociological literature suggests that a state agency's behavior (for example, its policies) depends on its organizational environment. This environment includes federal, state, and local agencies in the same functional area, as well as professional associations and interest groups.

Some political scientists have advocated the application of interorganizational theory to intergovernmental relations.[17] To our knowledge, however, no one has actually attempted such an enterprise. This book is the first empirical application of interorganizational theory to public policy. Since this theory's basic concepts are relatively new to political science, a chapter is devoted to discussing the entire body of interorganizational literature, its theoretical relevance to intergovernmental relations, and its applicability to public policy.

In recent sociological work, two different perspectives have been advanced to explain the formation of linkages between organizations.[18] One perspective, the exchange perspective, emphasizes cooperation and complementary goals as prerequisites for linkages. Interorganizational linkage is presumed to be voluntary and of mutual benefit. In contrast the power-dependency perspective adopts a conflict approach to the explanation of interorganizational relations. Within a network, organizations use their power to form links with more dependent organizations. The linkage benefits one member of the dyad more than the other; it is coerced, rather than consensually sought. Viewing the intergovernmental system as a series of functionally specific interorganizational networks, two types of federal strategies can be conceptualized to influence state policy: exchange and power-dependency. The federal government may attempt to establish complementary goals by encouraging professionalism, for example, in state agencies. Alternately it may create dependency by altering resource flows to state agencies and use its power over them to mandate pursuit of its chosen objectives.

Agencies' actions are best explained as a result of their interactions with other organizations. Interorganizational theory guides the analysis of those interactions. We conceive of federal strategies to control state agencies' actions as one organizational system's strategies to control another system of organizations. Interorganizational theory helps to understand the conditions under which different control strategies will be effective.

From the perspective of theories of interorganizational relations, Congress attempted to use the block grant to loosen state and local criminal-justice agencies' dependence on state and local governments. The Law Enforcement Assistance Administration's (LEAA) experience in attempting to influence state and local criminal-justice systems illustrates the problems associated with this block-grant approach to federal policymaking.

LEAA's block-grant program was established by the Omnibus Crime Control and Safe Streets Act of 1968, to increase the coordination and effectiveness of law-enforcement efforts at all levels of government. Under the act, planning and action funds are provided on the basis of a population formula to states, except for a small amount retained for LEAA's discretionary allocation. Each governor designates a state planning agency (SPA) to receive and disburse the federal money. The SPA submits an annual plan to LEAA outlining the state's problems and proposing how action funds should be allocated among competing demands in order to combat crime. After LEAA approves the plan (it has rejected only one in ten years), the SPA receives applications for specific projects from state and local governmental units or private organizations. The SPA staff and advisory board award money to projects, with the state providing a 10 percent match.

The SPA's role in granting funds is the outcome of the federal government's attempt to combine power-dependency and exchange strategies in influencing interorganizational networks. With small staffs (averaging twenty-six professional employees) and relatively little money (averaging less than 5 percent of the states' annual budgets for criminal-justice purposes), these agencies are supposed to carry out LEAA's mission.

The research identifies three goals of LEAA: achieving a balanced allocation of money among the three functions of corrections, courts, and police; stimulating innovation; and increasing coordination wtihin the criminal-justice system.[19] This study has evaluative and explanatory components: the extent to which SPAs are following federal directives (achieving LEAA's goals), and the reasons why LEAA and SPAs are not living up to their mandates. Interorganizational theory helps to answer the latter question by explaining the conditions under which federal control strategies work. The explanation of why LEAA does not meet its mandate is simultaneously an explanation of why the criminal-justice system works the way it does. Examination of these federal attempts to influence state and local criminal-justice agencies provides an opportunity to test the utility of the interorganizational perspective for understanding intergovernmental relations.

Chapters 5, 6, and 7 describe the results of these tests. First, patterns of functional allocation are analyzed: the amounts of money that each state subgrants to the police function, the courts functions, and the corrections function. LEAA's directive to the SPAs is that police should get less than they did in the past and the other functions more, thereby achieving balance among the functions. Second, instances of joint projects between functions are considered, and these projects are treated as evidence of system building or coordination. Third, six specific innovative programs are considered, two in each of the three functional categories: three are programs initiated by LEAA discretionary programs and followed up by the states; three are invented by the states themselves. The extent of each state's financial commitment to the six programs is examined.

Contributions to Research on Comparative State Politics
and Policy

This book contributes to comparative state research in several distinct ways. First, the politics-versus-economics debate, which has been emphasized to the detriment of the field, is avoided. The criminal-justice block grant is financed by the national government but the resource is allocated at the state level. State population, not wealth, determines each state's share of the block-grant funds. It is left to explain the *authoritative allocation of value* (that is, monetary grants): it is determined by political factors. The selection of an intergovernmental policy funded at the national level but implemented at the state level is deliberate, inasmuch as these partnerships are increasing over time and constitute a significant delivery mechanism. We are likely to learn more from one study of a block-grant program than from adding yet another study of a policy funded from the state's own resources to an already extensive literature. Revenue sharing was not selected because these monies are very difficult to trace through state and local budgets whereas block-grant funds are relatively easy to trace. Categorical grants, of course, allow so little state discretion that political explanations are inherently less promising.

The interorganizational approach is suitable for the substantive question: When states allocate funds supplied by the federal government, what factors determine who gets what, when, and how? The state's wealth is not a direct determinant. Political factors, especially organizational ones, can be determinative.

The inclusion of bureaucratic and organizational factors as political variables broadens the conception of political beyond the usual electoral and party measures. Not until 1976, in George Downs' study of juvenile community corrections, did anyone look systematically at the effect on a policy of bureaucratic, economic, and traditional political factors.[20] Some of the measures (such as the professionalism of SPA employees) allow a comparison of the results with his findings on the impact of agency personnel on policy.

The agency as the unit of analysis is focused on because it is the SPA that relates federal policy to the state. Fifty intergovernmental policy systems are compared. The system discussed in this book includes the SPA, LEAA, and the state and local criminal-justice agencies as political actors. Typically, comparative state studies treat states as isolated units for the purposes of analysis. Insofar as possible, interstate diffusion and federal influence are ignored in exploring the determinants of policy. States are analyzed as if they were closed political systems responding only to internal (intrastate) demands. In more recent years attacks on this practice (such as Rose's criticism) have led to a diminution in the number of comparative state studies.[21] The correct response to Rose's attack, however, is not to cease work but to undertake multilevel, intergovernmental, or contextual analysis. The intergovernmental system is an appropriate focus in an era when the federal government is a significant partner in producing state policy.

In this book policy is also conceptualized as a course of action to attack a problem. Therefore, analysis is not halted with an explanation of the *output* (with the amount of money LEAA sends to the state) but we examine the *policy action* (what states do with the money). Comparative state studies have often been criticized for relying on dimensions of policy that are easily quantifiable and readily available. Most often, these are monetary measures. One reason for their use is their availability. The more important reason for this reliance on expenditure data, however, is the conceptualization of policy as output. Now that scholarly attention is turning toward the implementation phase, measures of output alone no longer suffice. Increasingly, the state's role in implementation of federal policy will force students of state politics away from a focus on the laws enacted by state legislatures and toward a focus on state bureaucracies' action.

Contributions to Research on Public Policy

In several ways, this book contributes to the resolution of problems in public-policy research. Typically other research ignores the need and desire for a policy. Designs are cross-sectional and make narrow use of organizational theory.

The primary contribution is the incorporation of the concept of need for a particular policy. This may not appear to be such a revolutionary position but, to the best of our knowledge, no policy studies have developed measures of need. They implicitly assume that citizens always prefer more of everything and that the "best" government is the one that spends the most. In comparative state studies, authors worry about why states are laggard; in case studies, authors view a bill's passage as a virtue. If nothing else, the taxpayers' revolt of the late 1970s shows that at least some citizens want less government spendings. From their perspective, the best government is that which governs least.

Perhaps both scholars and activists would agree that the best government is one that accurately translates citizens' preferences (whether they be for more or less) into public policy. Godwin and Shepard have recently advocated a focus on *translation error,* the discrepancy between the observed policies of a political jurisdiction and the policies desired by its citizens.[22] Unfortunately, their article is stronger on the conceptual level than on the operational level. Since there are no relevant survey data on a state-by-state basis, it is not known how citizens' desires differ from one state to another.

For the policy examined in this book, a reasonable hypothesis is that citizens prefer more spending on criminal-justice policy where crime is severe. Therefore, the governments that are spending money on crime according to its incidence are translating citizens' demands accurately. Need for a policy (that is, severity of the problem), then, is a proxy measure for citizen demand.

Policy studies must take a longitudinal perspective, whether it be a comparative design over time or a historical case study.[23] The criminal-justice block-grant program was selected because it was one of the older ones, having been in existence ten years. The shortness of the time period does not permit time-series regression within each state, but relationships for an early period (1973) are compared with a later period (1976). In this way some sense of any changes in the organizational impact on policy is gained, while simultaneously providing more than a simple chronicle of the policy process.

The focus is on the agency as an organization. This approach is similar to that of most students of policy implementation. Most work on implementation has also relied on organization theory but has focused largely on intraorganizational factors. This intraorganizational focus derives from a desire to improve the organization's administrative process in order to achieve the desired outcome. In contrast, our interest is in how the federal government strategizes so as to get systems of delivery organizations to behave in a certain way; although our intent is not meliorative, our work is certainly relevant to any attempts to improve intergovernmental service delivery. The desired outcome is as much a function of interorganizational factors as of intraorganizational ones. Our approach, sometimes termed *macro implementation,*[24] is complementary to the *micro implementation* studies being done by students of the policy process. This book is concerned with the interactions of multiple organizational actors rather than with what happens within the delivery organization.

The three dependent variables (innovation, coordination, and functional allocation) were selected to reflect substantive and theoretical concerns. In addition to being LEAA's goals, however, these variables are standard topics for scholarly inquiry. Innovation has been widely studied in both sociology and political science.[25] An organization's motivation to cooperate is an important topic in organizational behavior.[26] The allocation of funds to different functions is also a standard topic in political science.[27] In each empirical chapter, extant literature on these phenomena informs us about how the overall theory should operate on this particular policy dimension. The results, in turn, have a broader impact beyond criminal justice policy.

For these reasons, the research for this book adds to the general literature on public policy as well as to that literature which compares states.

Contributions to Research on Intergovernmental Relations

The research for this book is most central to the field of intergovernmental relations. Scholarly writings on American federalism began, of course, with the institutional designers, James Madison and Alexander Hamilton. It was continued from a philosophical and legalistic perspective by Edward Corwin in the 1930s, William Anderson in the 1940s and 1950s, and Morton Grodzins in the 1960s.

The Intergovernmental-Relations Literature

A great deal of current literature by practitioners and scholars describes the American federal system and the changes brought about by the Creative Federalism of Lyndon Johnson and the New Federalism of Richard Nixon. In the late 1960s and early 1970s a frequent theme in this literature was the deleterious effects of the categorical grant-in-aid system on policy.[28] The New Federalism attempted to remedy these problems through the novel mechanisms of the block grant and revenue sharing (both general and special). General revenue sharing has been extensively monitored by a Brookings Institution research team; allocation of funds and their impact have been examined.[29] Thus, this one facet of the New Federalism is relatively well understood.

In contrast to the thoroughness of general revenue-sharing's study, however, block-grant programs have been the subjects of Advisory Commission on Intergovernmental Relations (ACIR) studies that tend more toward description than analysis.[30] For example, although the ACIR two-volume study of LEAA reports much data in frequency distributions, it lacks analysis of relationships. While this material has been invaluable it is the basis for a scientific study rather than a study itself. From the theoretical approach used in this book, propositions about the efficacy of different federal aid mechanisms in ensuring federal objectives were derived. Further, the research design allows evaluation of how one block grant has worked in fifty different settings. Thus this book can make a significant contribution to literature on the New Federalism by addressing the conceptual gaps that pervade the literature on block grants.

A perennial theme in the literature on American and comparative intergovernmental relations is the issue of whether the states or the national government should govern. Should the system be more decentralized or more centralized? In other societies, nation-state relations take the form of center-periphery conflicts and are exacerbated by the lack of political integration.[31] In the United States, much of the literature on nation-state relations is prescriptive and oriented toward state's rights. Still, there are several important questions identified in the prescriptive literature which can be investigated in the criminal-justice block-grant program.

From the state's perspective, an important issue is whether states have retained discretion over the allocation of crime-fighting dollars. The amount of interstate variation in the three policy variables serves as a measure of state allocation patterns. Analysis of state-level characteristics, such as need for the policy, answers the question of whether funds are allocated in accordance with state priorities.

From the national perspective, an important issue is whether central control can be exerted in a federal system. Several control mechanisms, already identified in the scholarly literature, will be evaluated in the study of the criminal-justice block grant. The professionalization of state and local employees is one potential means of federal control. Martha Derthick's insightful analysis of the public-assistance program in Massachusetts established the importance of professionalism as a control mechanism in the United States.[32] As professional social workers took the jobs of county workers in Massachusetts, they brought new attitudes about welfare clients, attitudes shared with federally employed social workers. Similarly, Beer has argued that technocrats are a force for centralization in all advanced societies.[33] Professionals share norms and values. Thus if professionals are employed at all levels of the federal system, similar behavior will be exhibited even in the absence of other incentives toward centralization.

In Derthick's study, professionalization of the public-assistance program consisted of requiring a college degree for caseworkers and the Masters of Social Work for higher ranking employees, thus drawing on the existing social-work profession. In seeking a similar result, LEAA had the more difficult job of creating a new profession of criminal-justice planning. Under the LEEP program (Law Enforcement Education Program), practitioners (police officers, courts, and corrections personnel) have received financial assistance amounting to $349,768,000 for college study. Funds totaling $25,768,000 have been provided to universities to begin criminal-justice graduate programs. One of the purposes of the research for this book was to examine the degree to which SPAs are staffed with criminal-justice professionals and professionalism's effect on the implementation of LEAA objectives.

Another potential means of federal control is money, particularly when federal dollars constitute a large proportion of a state agency's operating budget. The need for resources always makes an organization dependent on the source of such resources, according to the power-dependency approach to explaining interorganizational relations. If A has a resource that B needs, then A has power over B: B is dependent on A. If the federal agency (LEAA) controls funding that is essential to state criminal-justice agencies, then it has power over them; they are dependent on it.

At the same time that the federal agency is creating a dependency relationship with its state counterpart (SPA), it also attempts to make the state counterpart independent of the state through the resources of money and authority. Hale and Palley show that as the proportion of federal aid increases, state-agency officials become more independent of state political controls.[34] Derthick has argued that a state agency is more independent of state government if it is allowed discretion over federal funds rather than being a pass-through agency.[35] The fact that SPAs are new agencies and roughly 90 percent of the their funds are provided by LEAA makes the SPAs dependent on the federal government and independent of state government. The SPAs' funds, however, constitute only about 5 percent of the average state's criminal-justice budget. Other agencies in the states' criminal-justice systems are not highly dependent on the SPAs. They are not, therefore, very dependent on the federal government.

A third possible means of federal control is the requirement that a plan be submitted to the federal government by the recipient government, so that the former can ascertain compliance with national objectives before monies are allocated. Both block grants and project grants typically have this requirement. The criminal-justice block grant requires a lengthy plan annually from each state. Gamm has already suggested that interorganizational theory would be particularly useful for analyzing the intergovernmental planning process.[36]

Stinchcombe has also written about the conditions under which planning and the implementation of a plan is effective.[37] He has argued that effective implementation of a plan depends on the availability of liquid resources (money) and a lack of vested interests (interest groups). Interest groups can mobilize to block the performance of a plan. This barrier can, however, be overcome by large amounts of money. Interest groups respond to monetary incentives by ceasing to block the plan. The inclusion of the organizational strength of each function allows an investigation of his thesis.

Conceptualizations of Intergovernmental Systems

Presently, a resurgence of theoretical work in intergovernmental relations centers on the problem of institutional design in complex societies. The most influential group of scholars are those who take the perspective of public choice, such as Vincent Ostrom and his associates. Ostrom's purpose is the design of a federal system with fragmented authority and overlapping jurisdictions, whose quasi-markets would deliver services in the most efficient fashion.[38] His methodological individualism and concern with efficiency are alien to our theoretical position. We do agree, however, with his conception of the federal system as "a system of multiorganizational arrangements."[39] It is a conceptual advance beyond the metaphors (for example, layer cake or picket fence) that have populated the literature. His theoretical work corroborates our initial assertion that the key to understanding public policy lies in understanding the interaction of organizations.

Ostrom's theory of federalism has been applied to the study of problems of scale in public organizations. For example, E. Ostrom's large research project analyzed how the size and number of jurisdictions within a metropolitan area affect the supply of police services. Her goal was to find the optimum-sized police force.[40] His theory, however, is fairly restricted in its scope. Analysis is confined to public services, such as fire and police protection, available to a contiguous urban population.[41] This book discusses a delivery system that is not governed by a market mechanism. The block grant combines elements of hierarchy and authority as well as persuasion.[42]

There are other scholars, however, who advocate an interorganizational approach to intergovernmental realtions without the public-choice perspective— Kirlin, on the domestic side, and Hanf and Scharpf on the comparative side.[43] Two important points emerge from the Hanf and Scharpf volume that underscore and justify the approach in this book.

First, the inability of industrial societies to govern effectively can be directly traced to the difficulties of interorganizational policymaking. The collective capabilities of many participants located in separate organizations are essential to solve problems effectively. Securing their cooperation or imposing more general policy considerations on their actions is a major task of political systems in advanced economies. [44] Thus the organizational difficulties in implementing a block grant are part of a larger class of coordination problems in an organizationally-dense society.

Second, the editors call for a resolution of two competing research perspectives in intergovernmental policy studies—prescriptive or evaluative studies (such as the Ostroms') and positive or empirical studies explaining policymaking (such as this study). The selection of clearly identified policy goals as dependent variables will enable us to bridge the gap between the empirical theory and the need for prescriptive statements. On the basis of observed relationships, inferences can be made about the theory's success or failure as well as LEAA's success or failure. A program-evaluation study would just do the latter; a purely theoretical piece would only do the former.

For our purposes, Kirlin's work makes an important point. He suggests that the federal system be conceptualized as *articulated variety,* that is, flexible systems capable of joint action without a central dominant authority.[45] Rejecting Ostrom's emphasis on the nature of the good provided, he emphasized the choice of policy strategies as providing the structure of the federal system. Strategies can be ranged on a continuum of the degree of constraint: administrative strategies result in the most constrained systems because they stress centralized decision making and control; learning-system strategies (for example, block grants) result in the least constrained systems because they allow discretion by constituent units; organizational-environmental strategies result in systems of middling constraint. The investigation of a block-grant program will shed light on this generic class of learning-system strategies.

Conceptual work on the *emergent intergovernmental system* (Kirlin's term) is a very small and recent portion of all scholarship in the field. The Ostroms' work is the most developed, encompassing both theory and considerable empirical research. However, we favor the sociological reasoning that sees the basic interactions determining policy as organizational interactions. In fact, both Kirlin and Hanf and Scharpf refer to exchange and dependency notions, though neither author actually employs these concepts in research.

Notes

1. Advisory Commission on Intergovernmental Relations, *In Brief: The Intergovernmental Grant System: An Assessment and Proposed Policy* (Washington, D.C. U.S. Government Printing Office, no date), p. 26. The property tax constitutes 18 percent of state and local revenues combined and the sales tax 19 percent.

2. Others have identified increasing interdependence among all sectors of society as being characteristic of the post-industrial phase of development. See: Roger Benjamin, *The Limits of Politics* (Chicago: University of Chicago Press, 1980), p. 27.

3. Thomas R. Dye, *Politics, Economics, and the Public* (Chicago: Rand McNally, 1966).

4. Hugh Heclo, *Modern Social Politics in Britain and Sweden* (New Haven, Conn.: Yale University Press, 1974), p. 4.

5. Ibid.; George W. Downs, Jr., *Bureaucracy, Innovation, and Public Policy* (Lexington, Mass.: Lexington Books, D.C. Heath and Co., 1976).

6. Herbert A. Simon, *Administrative Behavior,* 2nd ed. (New York: The Free Press, 1957).

7. See, for example: Jeffrey L. Pressman and Aaron B. Wildavsky, *Implementation* (Berkeley: University of California Press, 1973).

8. John Sprague and Louis P. Westefield, "Campaign and Context Interaction" (Paper presented at the Midwest Political Science Association, Chicago, 1979).

9. Douglas Rose, "National and Local Forces in State Politics: The Implications of Multi-Level Policy Analysis," *American Political Science Review* 67 (December 1973):1162–1173.

10. George P. Greenberg, Jeffrey A. Miller, Lawrence B. Mohr, and Bruce C. Vladeck, "Developing Public Policy Theory: Perspectives from Empirical Research," *American Political Science Review* 71(December 1977):1532–1543; George W. Downs, Jr., and Lawrence B. Mohr, "Conceptual Issues in the Study of Innovation," *Administrative Science Quarterly* 21(December 1976):700–714.

11. Downs, 1976.

12. Andrew Shonfield, *Modern Capitalism* (New York: Oxford University Press, 1969); Robert R. Alford, *Health Care Politics* (Chicago: University of Chicago Press, 1975).

13. Terry Sanford, *Storm Over the States* (New York: McGraw-Hill, 1967); Deil S. Wright, "The States and Intergovernmental Relations," *Publius* 1(Winter 1972):7–68.

14. For example, James Q. Wilson, *Political Organizations* (New York: Basic Books, 1973).

15. This theoretical position was first advocated by James D. Thompson, *Organizations in Action* (New York: McGraw-Hill Book Co., 1967).

16. Shirley Terreberry, "The Evolution of Organizational Environments," *Administrative Science Quarterly* 12(September 1968):590–613.

17. John J. Kirlin, "Structuring the Intergovernmental System: An Appraisal of Conceptual Models and Public Politics" (Paper delivered at American Political Science Association meeting, New York, September 1978).

18. J. Kenneth Benson, "The Interorganizational Network as a Political Economy," *Administrative Science Quarterly* 20(June 1975):229–249; Stuart M. Schmidt and Thomas A. Kochan, "Interorganizational Relationships: Patterns and Motivations," *Administrative Science Quarterly* 22(June 1977):220–234.

19. Other studies focus on other goals of LEAA such as planning and evaluation: Malcolm Feeley and Austin D. Sarat, *Reforming Criminal Justice: The Crisis of Theory and Practice in the Law Enforcement Assistance Administration* (Minneapolis: University of Minnesota Press, forthcoming).

20. Downs, 1976.

21. Rose, 1973.

22. R. Kenneth Godwin and W. Bruce Shepard, "Political Processes and Public Expenditures: A Reexamination Based on Theories of Representative Government," *American Political Science Review* 70(December 1976):1127–1135.

23. Virginia Gray, "Models of Comparative State Politics: A Comparison of Cross-Sectional and Time Series Analyses," *American Journal of Political Science* 20(May 1976):235–256.

24. Paul Berman, "The Study of Macro- and Micro-implementation," *Public Policy* 26(Spring 1978):157–184.

25. Everett M. Rogers and F. Floyd Shoemaker, *Communication of Innovation,* 2nd ed. (New York: Free Press, 1971); Jack L. Walker, "The Diffusion of Innovations Among the American States," *American Political Science Review* 63(September 1969):880–899.

26. Michael Aiken and Jerald Hage, "Organizational Interdependence and Intraorganizational Structure," *American Sociological Review* 33(December 1968):912–931.

27. Dye, 1966.

28. See, for example, the director of the Advisory Commission of Intergovernmental Relations, William G. Golman, "The Role of the Federal Government in the Design and Administration of Intergovernmental Programs," in "Intergovernmental Relations in the United States," ed. Harry W. Reynolds, Jr. *Annals of the American Academy of Political and Social Science,* 359(May 1965):23–34.

29. Richard P. Nathan, Allen D. Manvel, Susannah E. Calkins, and Associates, *Monitoring Revenue Sharing* (Washington, D.C.: The Brookings Institution, 1975).

30. Advisory Commission on Intergovernmental Relations, *Safe Streets*

Reconsidered: The Block Grant Experience 1968-1975 (Washington, D.C.: Government Printing Office, 1977).

31. See: Sidney Tarrow, *Between Center and Periphery* (New Haven, Conn.: Yale University Press, 1977).

32. Martha Derthick, *The Influence of Federal Grants: Public Assistance in Massachusetts* (Cambridge, Mass.: Harvard University Press, 1970).

33. Samuel H. Beer, "Federalism, Nationalism, and Democracy in America," *American Political Science Review* 72(March 1978):19.

34. George E. Hale and Marion Lief Palley, "Federal Grants to the States: Who Governs?" *Administration and Society* 11(May 1979):3-26.

35. Derthick, 1970, p. 205.

36. Larry Gamm, "Planning in Administration," *Policy Studies Journal* 5(Autumn 1976):70-79.

37. Arthur L. Stinchcombe, "Social Structure and Politics," in *Macropolitical Theory, Handbook of Political Science,* Vol. 3, eds. Fred I. Greenstein and Nelson W. Polsby (Reading, Mass.: Addison-Wesley, 1975), pp. 557-622.

38. Vincent Ostrom, *The Intellectual Crisis in American Public Administration* (University, Ala.: University of Alabama Press, 1973); Vincent Ostrom, *The Political Theory of a Compound Republic* (Blacksburg, Va.: VPI and SU, Center for the Study of Public Choice, 1971).

39. Vincent Ostrom, "Some Problems in Doing Political Theory: A Response to Golembiewski's 'Critique'," *American Political Science Review* 71(December 1977):1512.

40. Elinor Ostrom, Roger B. Parks, and Gordon P. Whitaker, "Defining and Measuring Structural Variations in Interorganizational Arrangements," *Publius* 4(Fall 1974):88-108.

41. It has also been criticized by Golembiewski for methodological inelegance, questionable assumptions, and conflicting predictions; Robert T. Golembiewski, "A Critique of 'Democratic Administration' and Its Supporting Ideation," *American Political Science Review* 71(December 1977):1488-1507.

42. These three systems are contrasted in Charles E. Lindblom, *Politics and Markets* (New York: Basic Books, 1977).

43. Kirlin, 1978; Kenneth Hanf and Fritz W. Scharpf, eds., *Interorganizational Policy Making,* Sage Modern Politics Series, Vol. 1 (Beverly Hills, Calif.: Sage Publications, 1978).

44. Kenneth Hanf, "Introduction," in Hanf and Scharpf, 1978, p. 2.

45. Kirlin, 1978, p. 10.

2 Organizations, Environments, and Policymaking

Over the past several years, students of public policy have examined the impact of bureaucratic organizations on its formulation and implementation. Many studies in a variety of policy areas have found that bureaucratic structure and behavior constrain policymaking and implementation. Virtually all studies of public policy which examine bureaucracy's effect have focused on the organization itself as the unit of analysis. These studies have examined the impact of intraorganizational factors on the organization's policy outputs. Factors like personnel characteristics (for example, training and recruitment),[1] staff-line conflicts,[2] standard-operating procedures,[3] and cleavages between political appointees and career staff[4] have been explored as determinants of policy formulation and implementation. The relationships between bureaucratic organizations and their environments have received little attention in political science.[5] This is a serious deficiency of the literature on bureaucracy and public policy.

In organizational sociology, it is now widely accepted that an organization's structure and its members' behavior are contingent on characteristics of its environment. Technology is the other factor that is widely conceded to affect the organization's structure and functioning. James Thompson's work provides an excellent analysis of the environmental and technological determinants of organizational structure and process.[6] Thompson argues that organizations should be viewed as systems that employ various kinds of technologies to achieve their goals. At the most general level technologies specify cause-and-effect relationships that determine the organization's transformation of inputs into outputs. To assure the smooth and stable functioning of its technologies, an organization attempts to control the flow of inputs and disposition of outputs; that is, it attempts to control fluctuations in its environment.

Those portions of the environment that provide sources of inputs or markets for output are called an organization's *task environment*.[7] It consists of an organization's clients and consumers, suppliers of personnel, materials, or services, and competitors and regulators. Organizations seek to minimize uncertainty, and the task environment is the primary source of uncertainty. Organizations, therefore, seek to minimize their dependence on particular elements of the task environment and uncertainty about elements' actions. Thompson outlines a variety of strategies that organizations employ to reduce uncertainty about, and dependence on, elements of the task environment: "sealing off" core technologies; buffering environmental influences by stockpiling inputs and outputs; smoothing out fluctuations in input and output; anticipating fluctuations; rationing.[8] These strategies for dealing with the environment are reflected in the structure and processes of the organization.[9] The contingencies and constraints presented by the organization's task environments are determinants of its structure.

The impact of bureaucracy on public policy cannot be fully explained without examining the relationship between organizations and their task environments. Without an examination of the environments of bureaucratic organizations, the policies that the organizations pursue and the behavior of their members cannot be understood.

In a seminal work, Emery and Trist suggest a four-fold typology of organizational environments: the placid, randomized environment; the placid, clustered environment; the disturbed, reactive environment; the turbulent field, characterized by large, linked sets of organizations.[10] They argue that organizational structure will adapt to the particular environment in which the organization exists. Building on this argument, Terreberry argues that there has been a succession or evolution in the environments of most organizations, moving from the placid, randomized to the turbulent-field environment.[11] She argues that as societies become more organizationally dense, the task environments of organizations increasingly consist of other organizations. Other organizations, therefore, are likely to be important determinants of the structure and process of any single organization that one might examine. Terreberry's argument suggests that, in examining any particular public organization, it is important to examine the impact of the organizations that constitute its task environment. It is necessary to examine its *organization set*—the organizational actors in its task environment.[12] For this reason, special care is taken to examine theories of organization-environment relations that emphasize the effect of interorganizational linkages on organizational structure and process.

It is particularly important to consider the effect of interorganizational relations when examining intergovernmental relations in general and LEAA's impact on state and local criminal-justice systems in particular. As scholars have already noted, intergovernmental relations are increasingly dominated by the interactions of local, state, and federal bureaucracies operating within functionally defined areas.[13] The administrative portion of the intergovernmental system can be conceptualized as a series of functionally defined systems of interacting agencies. LEAA's administration of federal block-grant funds certainly conforms to this characterization. The use of block-grant funds is determined by the interactions among the federal LEAA, state planning agencies (SPAs), and police departments, correction agencies, and courts at the state and local levels. Prospects for rationally setting and achieving federal, state, and local policy goals may be largely a function of the characteristics of these organizational interactions.

At this point it is necessary to define several terms that will be used through-out the remainder of this book. *Agency* refers to any public bureaucratic organ-ization that is part of the administrative apparatus of government. LEAA, state, and local police departments are all examples of agencies. By *unit of govern-ment*, nonbureaucratic, typically elective, institutions of government at all levels are meant. Congress, state legislatures, governors' offices, and mayors' offices are all referred to as units of government. An *organizational system* is defined as a set of agencies (within some defined area of government) with the same functional task. For example, the police departments in a state can be con-sidered an organizational system. For other purposes, the entire criminal-justice system in a state is defined as an organizational system. Generally, it is assumed that these agencies constitute a system to the extent that they share the same task environment, compete for the same resources (for example, budgetary allocations for local, state, and federal units of government), and deal with the same set of clients. As a set of agencies shares more and more aspects of its task environment, their organizational system will become more tightly coupled. The tightness of a system's coupling is the degree to which changes in the task en-vironment affect all agencies in the system in an identical fashion. In a tightly coupled system, any change in the task environment will have the same effect on all agencies in the system. In a loosely coupled system, agencies will have greater latitude to strategize about or, in some cases, to ignore changes in the task environment.[14]

The term *change-agent organization* is taken from Sutton.[15] A change-agent organization is an agency that is charged by another agency or unit of govern-ment with the task of altering the policies pursued by agencies within a par-ticular organizational system. For example, SPAs are change-agent organizations created at the direction of LEAA and state units of government to alter the policies pursued by state and local criminal-justice agencies.

There are two general ways in which change-agent organizations can alter the structure of and policies pursued by agencies within an organizational sys-tem. These two strategies define the modes of control and coordination within the intergovernmental system. First, by altering factors of the task environment of an organizational system, the change-agent organization can change the costs and benefits of potential and present policies pursued by agencies. If the change is sufficiently severe, the change-agent organization may cause agencies to alter their practices. Typically, this strategy would involve altering the criteria for allocating money and authority to agencies within the system. Second, the change-agent organization may seek to penetrate the agencies themselves, and alter intraorganizational decision making. By altering the decisional premises used by agency personnel, it would be possible to change policy without altering factors of the task environment. Organizational members would view the exist-ing task environment differently and would therefore respond to it with new policies.[16] This strategy might involve requiring that agencies be staffed with professionals, who will view the task environment in a particular way. LEAA has employed both of these modes of control and coordination in its attempts to influence state and local criminal-justice systems.

Theories of Organization-Environment Interaction

Two different perspectives have come to dominate the study of organization-environment relations: selection and adaptation. Both approaches begin by assuming that organizational structure and process is conditioned by characteristics of the task environment. They differ dramatically, however, in their conclusions. The approaches suggest, therefore, two quite different logics for constructing an organizationally-based theory that can be used to explain American policymaking.

The adaptation perspective analyzes the ways in which organizations adapt to the constraints and contingencies imposed by their task environments. Insofar as this environment is dominated by other organizations, the adaptation approach examines interorganizational relations that are formed within a particular organizational system. The approach emphasizes the ways in which organizations use and strategize about interorganizational relations in order to minimize uncertainty and dependence. The selection (or population ecology) approach focuses on the demands created by a particular task environment rather than on organizational responses to these demands. Instead of a focal organization, this approach examines the types of organizations that are selected by a particular set of environmental demands. The selection approach does not emphasize the importance of the succession of task environments as described by Terreberry, nor does it consider the implications of the increasing domination of task environments by organizational actors.

Both the selection and adaptation approaches have important, albeit differing, implications for the study of bureaucracy's role in public-policy formulation and implementation. They are particularly useful in examining the conditions under which change occurs in the policy outputs of government agencies. Therefore, both approaches are received in detail. The adaptation perspective is drawn on to examine LEAA's attempts to influence state and local criminal-justice systems.

The Selection Approach

The selection approach to the study of organization-environment relations assumes that organizations' ability to change and adapt to their environments is limited.[17] Two conditions are necessary for the selection approach to be applicable to a population of organizations. First, organizations must have a low adaptive potential. There must be good reasons for assuming that they cannot change their structures fast enough to respond to changing environmental demands. Hannan and Freeman, for example, argue that the literature on organizations uniformly concludes that there is a tendency toward inertia in large organizations.[18] Given this tendency to resist change, they argue that it is profitable to examine which kinds of organizations are selected by particular types of task environments. Second, the task environment must exert strong pressures on organizations. Organizations that fail to meet environmental demands will not survive. If these two conditions are met, attention turns to the types of organizational structures that are selected by a particular environment and away from any concern with structural adaptation. In such a case, it is the environment that is of primary importance and not organizational response to that environment.

In the selection approach, the unit of analysis is not a focal organization but a population of organizations in a particular environment. Aldrich and Pfeffer describe the logic of the environment's selection of an organizational type as "best-suited" to its demands.[19] The description is borrowed from Campbell's work on the application of evolutionary models to all types of social structures.[20] First, some initial structural variation is assumed to exist in the population of organizations under consideration. Second, the task environment provides a "consistent selection criterion," which leads some variations to survive and others to be eliminated. Such a selection process for organizations is best illustrated by the competitive market. The consistent selection criterion is internal efficiency, and only those firms with the appropriate structure to produce marketable goods efficiently survive. Third, the "selected out" alternative is retained, reproduced, and diffused. Thus in any "distinguishable environmental configuration, one finds in equilibrium only that organizational form optimally adapted to the demands of the environment."[21] This equilibrium state is not reached through the changes that individual organizations make in their structures but through the survival of those organizations that already possess structural arrangements appropriate to the environment's selection criterion.

The primary utility of the selection approach in the study of public policy is as a heuristic device. It suggests that the federal system can be viewed as a variety of environments within which organization systems of government agencies exist. Two sources of environmental demand exist within any particular environment: those units of government or agencies that control scarce resources (for example, budgets and grants of authority), and client and constituent groups that make demands for particular mixes of goods and services.[22] As these demands change the kinds of agencies within a given organizational system also change. Environmentally appropriate agencies will be selected out while inappropriate ones will fail to survive.

This view of government agencies in a federal system is plausible when applied to the area of criminal justice. Through LEAA the federal government is attempting to alter the task environment of state and local criminal-justice agencies. Using the three steps of the population-ecology selection process, it is possible to speculate about the effects of LEAA's actions. We begin with a given population of state and local criminal justice agencies. Because they exist in state and locally determined task environments, their structures and behaviors are likely to be diverse.[23] The second stage of the process occurs when the federal government, through LEAA, attempts to influence the composition of the population of state and local criminal-justice agencies. It seeks to construct a population in which the majority of the organizations are professionalized, oriented to planning, committed to LEAA-desired innovations, and amenable to coordination. Block-grant funds are intended to be distributed on the basis of consistent selection criteria. These criteria should uniformly alter the task environments of criminal-justice agencies. By using criteria such as innovation, cooperation, and professionalization to determine the allocation of block-grant funds, LEAA is attempting to choose certain kinds of criminal-justice agencies. Only those agencies conforming to standards set by LEAA will continue to receive large amounts of discretionary block-grant funds. If the federal government is successful, the selected structures for criminal-justice agencies would be retained and diffused throughout state and local criminal-justice systems.

While the population-ecology approach is useful as a heuristic device, its utility is limited. For three reasons government agencies do not meet the assumptions of the model. First, to systematically apply the approach, it must be possible to assume that the task environment places sufficient pressure on a population of organizations to actually select certain types and cause other types to disappear. The essence of *incrementalism* as the guiding principle of budgeting, however, is that these hard decisions are never made.[24] Agencies are rarely eliminated in the budgetary process.

Second, the population-ecology approach implies that the pressures exerted by the environment are not only severe but also consistent. Demands must be structured so as to allow only a limited number of structural types to survive. In an environment where demands do not pull consistently in the same direction, latitude exists for strategizing by organizational members. The selection approach, however, assumes that such strategizing is unimportant. In a federal system there is a good deal of independence between levels of government. The demands created by such diversity will usually be inconsistent.

Third, Hannan and Freeman note sufficient inertia must exist in the structure of organizations to ensure that the environment will select types of organizations, rather than having organizations adapt and change their structure.[25] Although there may be a good deal of inertia in the structure of government agencies, there are compelling reasons for avoiding the assumption that these organizations do not change. By focusing solely on the environment, this approach ignores the internal processes of organizations. In ignoring these processes, it ignores what may be of primary importance for explaining the policy outputs of public organizations.

In a competitive market these internal processes may be assumed to be irrelevant. Despite what goes on within organizations, the market determines which organizations will be successful in acquiring resources and disposing of outputs. Only those organizations that satisfy market requirements survive. In the public sector, however, organizations do not compete with one another to dispose of their outputs (that is, public policies). Similarly, they do not compete, except for marginal increments in budget allocations, for their resource inputs. Changes in the policies produced by public organizations cannot be attributed solely to environmental pressures. Rather, changes are the product of both environmental demands and the strategic choices of organizational members.[26]

In the public sector the influence of the organizations in an agency's environment is a function of the extent to which they can affect the direction of its strategic choices. This effect can occur in two ways: by altering factors in the task environment and thereby changing the costs and benefits of certain policies; by altering the premises used by decision-makers but without changing the organization's task environment. Thus the use of block grants by the federal government is not really an attempt to force some criminal-justice agencies "out of business" and allow others to survive. It is a device to affect all criminal-justice agencies to the greatest extent possible and alter their decision making so that they produce policies more in keeping with federal standards in criminal justice.

To fully examine this process of penetration, the adaptation of the focal organization must be looked at—its strategic responses to environmental demands—as well as the selective processes operating in its task environment. While looking at the alteration of the criminal-justice agencies' task environments by the federal government (that is, at factors stressed by the selection approach), the response or adaptation of the agencies to these alterations must also be examined. In order to develop a specific set of propositions for examining LEAA's influence over state and local criminal-justice agencies, it is necessary to turn to the other major approach to the study of organization-environment relations—the adaptation perspective.

The Adaptation Approach

According to Hannan and Freeman, the adaptation approach dominates the study of interorganizational relations and general organization theory.[27] It focuses on the ways in which a focal organization, or system of organizations, responds and adapts to the contingencies and constraints presented by its task environment.

The assumptions of the adaptation approach constrast with the assumptions of the selection approach. First, the adaptation approach does not assume that severe and consistent pressures are exerted by the environment, resulting in the survival of only a limited range of organizational structures. Rather, many different types of organizational structures may be compatible with the demands of a given task environment. Second, in contrast to the selection approach's assumption of organizational inertia, the adaptation approach assumes that organizations strategize over the ways in which they will respond to their task environment's demands. As the task environment comes to be dominated by other organizations, the relationships established between the focal organization and members of its organization set become increasingly important; interorganizational linkages are consciously and strategically formed.

Within the adaptation perspective, two explanations are generally offered for the formation of interorganizational linkages: exchange and power-dependence. The *exchange* explanation emphasizes cooperation and complementary goals as prerequisites for the formation of interorganizational linkages. It assumes that organizations establish relationships with other organizations when members of both organizations perceive "mutual benefits or gains from interacting."[28] For example, in their examination of health-care-delivery agencies, Levine and White found that consensus over organizational domain was a prerequisite for the formation of interorganizational linkages.[29] In short, the exchange explanation assumes that, given complementary goals, organizations will cooperate to achieve them.

The power-dependence explanation for the formation of interorganizational linkages adopts a conflict approach. In this view organizations use their influence or power within a particular task environment to form links with other organizations. These links are engineered to provide the initiating organization with a steady supply of needed resources. Power and the interdependency among organizations, therefore, determine the type and the number of interorganizational relationships that will be found in any set of organizations.[30]

Schmidt and Kochan argue that the power-dependence and exchange explanations of interorganizational linkages form two ends of a continuum.[31] They suggest that neither explanation is adequate when used in isolation because any given organization is likely to have relationships of both types. In this view organizations segment their environment and employ different strategies for dealing with each segment.[32]

It is important to note the extent to which the adaptation perspective differs from the population-ecology (or selection) approach. The latter perspective never examines factors like organizational strategies or the ways in which different organizations perceive or "enact" their task environments.[33] Yet, in the public realm, these factors influence the structure and policies of agencies in any given task environment.

Influencing Agencies in the Intergovernmental System:
Exchange and Power Dependence

The selection and adaptation approaches can provide important insights into the problems involved in controlling bureaucratic organizations. The selection approach implies that the control of agencies depends on the ability of governmental units to define the prerequisites for organizational survival. Given organizational inertia, the only way to control organizations is to be certain that undesirable agencies are eliminated (for example, through sunset laws and strict funding limits) and to create environments that only allow desired kinds of agencies to survive.

The adaptation perspective implies that less severe control mechanisms may be successful. Through manipulation of critical resources in the task environment, government units can attempt to influence the strategies that an agency pursues in adapting to environmental demands. Government units can also exert influence by controlling the kinds of premises used by decision makers in agencies and the kinds of persons recruited to the agencies.

Organizations are faced with many, often conflicting, demands from their environment. The task of organizational managers is to determine which of these demands the organization will meet. Organizations selectively respond to elements in their task environments. The process of selecting the salient aspects of a task environment is a subjective one. Even when faced with the same "objective" task environments, organizations do not attend to the same aspect. The portion of the task environment to which a particular organization responds is called the *enacted environment*.[34] To the extent that government units control portions of an agency's enacted environment or can influence the definition of that environment, the agency will be responsive to the government unit's demands. Within any organizational system, however, different agencies may choose to respond to different demands in the task environment; in this case, the government unit's control will differ from agency to agency. Thus it is important to analyze the strategies employed by government units for controlling organizational systems and the likely effects of these strategies.

Schmidt and Kochan's work is helpful in analyzing control strategies employed by government units and attempts to exert federal influence over the policymaking of state and local agencies. The federal government may pursue two different strategies for influencing state and local policymaking. It may pursue an exchange strategy by attempting to establish a set of complementary goals for state and local agencies or a power-dependency strategy by establishing standards for the use of federal money handed over to state and local agencies.

Clark's early study of federal attempts to influence local educational policy is an excellent example of the use of an exchange strategy.[35] Committees of highly prestigious educators were created to serve as links between the federal government and local school boards. These committees established voluntary curriculum standards which were widely adopted throughout the country. Clark suggests that the program was successful because of the committees' high prestige in the educational community. In exchange terms, the presence of the committees made local school boards view the adoption of new standards as being in their own interest as well as in the interest of the federal government. Power and dependency were not involved in the establishment of the new standards. Rather, organizations at the local level saw it as in their own interests to alter their structure and policies in order to consider new sets of standards. Clark argues that, by establishing this consensus over goals, the program was highly successful—despite the absence of either federal regulations or large expenditures.

Exchange is one possible strategy that the federal (or any level of) government can employ to influence the policies pursued by operating agencies. LEAA's emphasis on the development of criminal-justice planning, for example, demonstrates the use of an exchange strategy akin to that described by Clark. By encouraging the staffing of SPAs with criminal-justice planners, LEAA attempted to develop *change-agent organizations,* which were expected to have high prestige among state and local criminal-justice agencies. They could, therefore, influence these agencies' decision-making processes. In addition, SPAs' professionalism was expected to facilitate cooperation between LEAA and the SPAs themselves, due to the shared values of the professionals in both organizational settings.

Professionalization is a way of ensuring uniformity among agencies in the way that they enact their task environments. Because they share the same norms and values, criminal-justice planners at all levels of government and in all types of agencies are likely to regard the same aspects of their task environments as being important. If LEAA's strategy is successful, criminal-justice agencies staffed by planners will be receptive to the types of policies desired by LEAA itself. Professionalization is a way of controlling agencies' policies without manipulating the task environment to the extent implied by either the power-dependence strategy or the selection approach.

The power-dependence strategy for influencing state and local policymaking is quite different from the exchange strategy. It involves altering the flow of resources into the state and local organizational system. Benson calls this strategy a form of manipulation undertaken to change the program priorities and technological commitments of agencies.[36] The power-dependence strategy is based on the assumption that organizations are resource-seeking entities that tend to be influenced by organizations in their environments which control critical resources.

Pfeffer and Salancik identify three factors that determine the degree of dependence that exists between organizations and, thus, the degree of power that one organization may have over another.[37] First, the importance of the resource at stake affects dependence. The more important the resource and the more of it that comes from the organization in question, the greater the dependence. Second, the number of alternative sources for the resource affects the degree of dependence. The fewer the alternatives, the greater the dependence. Third, the extent to which the granting organization has discretion over the allocation and use of the resource affects dependence. The greater the discretionary control, the greater the dependence. It is important to note that, while these three conditions determine the degree of dependence and power, organizations are expected to resist such dependent relationships. Organizations are assumed to seek autonomy and thus pursue strategies to limit their dependence on other organizations. The adaptation approach assumes that organizations strategize to achieve autonomy. This is in marked contrast to the selection approach's indifference to the issue.

Pfeffer and Salancik's discussion has direct relevance for analyzing public policy in a federal system. We assume that the resources most often at stake in the federal system are money and authority. A particular agency is dependent on another agency or unit of government to the extent that the latter is responsible for granting a high percentage of the focal agency's budget or controls its grant of authority. The extent of dependence increases as the unit of government in question is the only source of funding or authority available to the agency. Finally, and perhaps most importantly, dependence on the granting unit of government is determined by its discretion over the allocation of funds or authority. If the granting unit is required by statute to grant money or authority regardless of the policy pursued by the receiving agency, then the amount of influence exerted by the grantor is likely to be minimal.

For the federal government to establish a successful power-dependence relationship with state and local agencies, two conditions must be met. A dependence relationship must be created, and the maintenance of any new resource flow must be conditional on the adoption of specific standards. The first condition is met if the state and local agencies receive a large amount of their input resources from the federal government and they cannot control federal decisions about these resources' allocations. If the amount of money at stake is a very small percentage of an agency's budget, there is little incentive for it to alter its policies. The federal government must make the agency dependent on federal funds (or on the federal grants of authority over a policy) for this strategy to succeed.

In an area like criminal justice, where federal, state, and local levels of government are involved in providing money and granting authority to operating agencies, establishing such a dependent relationship between criminal-justice agencies and the federal government may be extremely difficult. Pfeffer and Salancik, for example, note that it is much more difficult for any one organization to exert influence over a system with dispersed resources than in one with concentrated resources.[38] Using the selection (or population ecology) approach, Hannan and Freeman reach the same conclusion.[39] They suggest that when the demands of a larger system (for example, the federal government) are added to a local system of demands that affect organizations, the diversity of environmentally appropriate organizational types would be expected to increase. This increase would result unless the larger system's constraints replaced rather than simply augmented the constraints of the local system.

It thus becomes necessary for the federal government to establish dependency relationships with operating agencies in order to be sure that when federal and state or local standards conflict, the agencies will be responsive to federal standards. Hale and Palley's study of the influence of federal grants on state agencies illustrates the effects of a dependency relationship between the federal government and state or local agencies.[40] They found that as the amount of federal aid increased as a percentage of an agency's operating budget, agency officials became more independent of state political controls. Freeing agencies from the control of state and local units of government is not, however, a guarantee that the agencies will then be responsive to the federal government. In addition to establishing a minimal dependency relationship, the federal government must be able to attach effective conditions to its grant of money or authority. In the absence of such conditions, the federal government only establishes an independent network of agencies that will not necessarily alter existing policies. In such a case, the federal government fails to affect the decision making of organizational policymakers. Agencies are likely to use their power or influence to maximize their share of any newly available input resources but are unlikely to change their policies without pressure or incentive to do so.

Agencies' tendencies to maximize their share of the inflow of resources is demonstrated in the allocation of block-grant funds to state and local criminal-justice systems. Competition for these funds among functional categories (police, courts, and corrections) has been fairly intense. Indeed, Congress has had to compensate for the organizational strength of the police by earmarking funds for other categories.

Both the selection and adaptation perspectives imply that if influence is based on manipulation of the task environment by altering criteria for allocating money or authority, stringent guidelines for the use of these resources are extremely important. The selection approach suggests that in the absence of such guidelines, the task environment does not provide any selection mechanisms for discarding agencies with structures inconsistent with the ends of the granting units. As demonstrated by the Hale and Palley study, federal altering of agencies' task environments can destroy the ability of state and local units of government to control agencies' task environments and thus their ability to control the agencies. In such a case, the result of federal manipulation of the task environment is increased independence of operating agencies from any form of political control at the state, local, or federal level.

The adaptation perspective emphasizes a different set of factors but reaches the same conclusions about the creation of new sources of funding or authority without any controls attached to the use of those resources. In such a case, the federal government does not control the agency, while reducing the extent of local and state control. The number of organizational policies consistent with survival increase, and organizational policymakers are much freer to make policy without considering the preferences of other organizations. In effect, the importance of the environment decreases and the agency's autonomy increases. In a general sense, this problem of providing both resources and requirements for the use of those resources accounts for the difficulty of achieving legislative and executive control of the activities of bureaucratic agencies. For this reason the internal structure of organizations becomes important for understanding public policy. To the extent that the environment created by legislatures and executives does not provide clear-cut survival requirements (that is, an extremely limited number of strategies that are consistent with survival requisites), the strategic choices of agency decision makers become more important and less constrained. However, professionalization is a possible means of controlling agencies in the absence of a strictly controlled task environment.

There are important implications for evaluating the alternative strategies that the federal government has traditionally employed to influence state and local agencies. Three methods have been used, all of which manipulate resource flows into state and local organizational systems: categorical grants-in-aid, block grants, and revenue sharing. These methods differ dramatically in their potential for establishing successful power-dependence relationships between operating agencies and granting units of government.

Categorical grants-in-aid meet both conditions for a successful power-dependency strategy. Due to generally liberal federal-matching formulas, the grant provides a significant share of an agency's budget for a particular policy. Thus dependence is established and there are few alternative sources of money to which the agency can turn (assuming that the grants-in-aid programs are reasonably coordinated). More importantly, federal guidelines are specific about the use of the grant money. The alternatives for agency action are limited.

General revenue sharing has quite different implications when viewed from the perspective of organization-environment theory. Instead of giving money directly to operating agencies, the federal government delegates the allocative responsibilities to state and local units of government. Manipulation of existing organizational systems is left to these state and local units. In this way the federal government provides increased resources but does not lessen existing control by state and local units of government. One bit of evidence for the assertion that general revenue sharing does not alter the power relationships that exist between state and local units of government is provided by Caputo and Cole.[41] In a study of city allocation of general revenue-sharing monies, they found that the additional revenues were allocated by city governments to functions in the same proportions that already existed in budgets. Thus while general revenue sharing eliminates the federal role in controlling the task environments of state and local agencies, it does not loosen control that already exists at the state and local level. State and local units can use federal money to establish power-dependence relationships with operating agencies and thereby control them.

Block grants, the third way for the federal government to aid state and local governments, meet only one of the two conditions for a successful power-dependency strategy. The federal government can provide a sizeable proportion of an agency's budget, thereby lessening its dependence on state and local government units. To the extent that block grants are provided without specific guidelines for their use, however, their effect is likely to be the creation of agencies that are independent of state, local, or federal governmental units. Since block grants do not provide specific criteria that force the agency to use the funds in a manner mandated by outside units, they are likely to be used in ways chosen by bureaucrats within the agency.

Interorganizational Theory and the Law
Enforcement Assistance Administration

Some general propositions can be formulated about the probable outcomes of various federal attempts to influence state and local organizational systems. These propositions are used for the analysis of LEAA's influence over state and local criminal-justice systems; however, they are meant to be generally applicable to attempts by any unit of government to alter the policies pursued by existing agencies.

The interactions between three critical factors—dependence, organizational strength and the professionalism of both change-agent organizations (SPAs) and state and local agencies—are the basis for these propositions.

Dependence refers to the extent to which a focal agency or organizational system receives critical resources from a particular source. In the public sector it is clear that budgetary allocations are the critical resource sought by agencies.[42] This is particularly true among service-oriented government agencies, which are typically labor intensive.

Organizational strength refers to the degree to which an existing agency or organizational system has already established independence from the demands of governmental units in its task environment. It refers to the clout of the agency or organizational system and reflects its ability to resist federal attempts to impose outside standards on it. Pfeffer and Salancik, for example, suggest that organizations have three alternatives when faced with new demands from their task environments.[43] They can adapt to the demands, they can ignore the demands, or they can attempt to alter the task environments. The stronger an agency or an organizational system, the more likely it is to be able to success-fully pursue the latter two strategies.

The *professionalism* of change-agent organizations and state and local agencies indicates the degree to which an exchange strategy can be successful. Highly professionalized personnel in agencies are likely to share important values with professional personnel at other levels of government. If an exchange strategy is successful, these shared professional values will lead to similar preferences for policies. In the study in this book, it is predicted that if an exchange strategy is operative, highly professionalized SPAs and state and local agencies are more likely to pursue goals set by LEAA than are less professionalized SPAs and state and local agencies.

Before describing the specific propositions that guide the analysis, it is necessary to elaborate on the indicators used for evaluating the success or failure of federal strategies to influence state and local criminal-justice agencies. It was assumed that the state and local agencies are primarily influenced by state and local politics. Further, it was assumed that the current allocation of resources to those agencies will be primarily determined by past alloca-tions of resources: incrementalism is the guiding force for resource allocation. In order to conclude that federal efforts to influence these agencies have been successful, three things must be observed. First, the grip of incrementalism must be broken. Second, changes in the pattern of resource allocation must be related to the policy preferences of federal actors. In order to conclude that the federal government has successfully established a dependent rela-tionship with state and local agencies, it is necessary to observe a lessening of state and local influence and an increase in federal influence. Finally, in-sofar as the goal of LEAA is a more rational allocation of resources according to the state's own crime needs and resources, it is expected that the agencies with the most need for a particular policy are the most committed to that policy.

Proposition 1. Where the dependence of state and local agencies on federal funds is low, change in response to federal directives is unlikely.

Where the incentives for organizational change are minimal, no change is likely. Where the potential federal contribution is only a small percentage of an agency's operating budget, the agency is likely to follow the second of Pfeffer's and Salancik's strategies: ignore the new demand. It is unlikely that a small amount of new resources will lead an agency to either accede to federal demands for policy change (assuming they are made known) or to mobilize its strength to alter these demands. When the size of block-grant funds at the dis-cretion of SPAs is small, state and local criminal-justice agencies are unlikely to accept the funds and accede to federal standards or to mobilize their strength to gain control over the new resources without acceding to federal standards (that is, altering the task environment).

Proposition 2. Where dependence of state and local agencies on federal funds is high, the potential for change in accordance with federal goals is high, but the potential for agency mobilization to gain control over those resources without acceding to federal guidelines is also high.

A large amount of new federal money or grants of authority introduced into an existing organizational system of state and local agencies constitutes a threat to the status quo and hence to the domains of agencies within that system. As the amount of money introduced increases, it constitutes an environmental change that agencies cannot ignore. Two outcomes are possible. First, the agencies can mobilize their organizational strength to maximize their share of new resources while simultaneously trying to alter or ignore the requirements attached to the new money. In this way, they can try to maintain their existing set of policies. One manifestation of this strategy is lobbying Congress on behalf of various state and local agencies in an attempt to alter the amount of LEAA funds allocated to their criminal-justice area. Second, the agencies can take the money and adopt new policies in accord with the federal standards.

Proposition 3. Where the professionalism of SPAs and state and local criminal-justice agencies is high, federal standards are likely to be incorporated into the policy decisions of these agencies. Where the professionalism of SPAs and state and local criminal-justice agencies is low, federal standards are unlikely to be incorporated into the policy decisions of these agencies.

Proposition 3 concerns the effectiveness of the exchange strategy as a means for penetrating the decision-making processes of agencies. LEAA has used professionalism (for example, development of criminal-justice planning as a profession) as a means for building its prestige. In this context professionalism may be viewed from two different perspectives. First, it creates a set of shared norms and values for federal decision makers and members of the change-agent organizations (SPAs). In testing proposition 3, the relationship is examined between an SPA's professionalization and the extent to which the policies that it pursues are consistent with LEAA's guidelines. Second, professionalization is a way of influencing agencies at the state and local level. It is expected that professionalization of personnel within these agencies increases the likelihood that they will pursue policy goals consistent with the aims of the professionals within LEAA and the SPAs.

Proposition 4. Maximum compliance with federal goals will be obtained when both exchange and power-dependence strategies are operative.

In this proposition, an interactive relationship between exchange and power-dependence strategies is anticipated. Schmidt and Kochan suggest that the empirical relationship between power-dependence and exchange strategies has general implications for policymakers in a federal system. Policymakers seeking to change interorganizational relations must focus on the problems of coordination (exchange) and the distribution of power.[44]

It is important to understand the relationship between exchange and power-dependence strategies, especially where federal block grants are employed. If the block grant creates a dependent relationship between the federal government and state or local agencies, the potential for changing the organizational system is present. In order to ensure that agencies respond to federal influence in their actual policy decisions, however, it is necessary to overcome their tendency to maximize their share of the grant while retaining existing policies. In the absence of authoritative federal guidelines, the prestige of the change-agent organization becomes critical. It is the only mechanism that can induce changes consistent with federal policies through voluntary cooperation founded on the creation of complementary organizational goals. An exchange strategy is most effective once a dependency relationship has been established. In the absence of a successful exchange strategy, the effect of block grants is likely to be the increased independence of state and local agencies from the control of any units of government.

Notes

1. See, for example: John A. Armstrong, *The European Administrative Elite* (Princeton, N.J.: Princeton University Press, 1973; Hugh Heclo, *Modern Social Politics in Britain and Sweden* (New Haven, Conn.: Yale University Press, 1974).

2. See, for example: William A. Lucas and Raymond H. Dawson, *The Organizational Politics of Defense* (Pittsburgh: International Studies Association, 1974).

3. See, for example: Graham T. Allison, *The Essence of Decision* (Boston: Little, Brown and Co., 1971).

4. See, for example: Lee Rainwater and William L. Yancey, *The Moynihan Report and the Politics of Controversy* (Cambridge, Mass.: The MIT Press, 1970); Francis E. Rourke, *Bureaucracy, Politics and Public Policy* (Boston: Little, Brown and Co., 1976), part 1.

5. For a notable exception see: George W. Downs, Jr., *Bureaucracy, Innovation, and Public Policy* (Lexington, Mass.: Lexington Books, D.C. Heath and Co., 1976).

6. James D. Thompson, *Organizations in Action* (New York: McGraw-Hill Book Co., 1967).

7. William R. Dill, "Environment as an Influence on Managerial Autonomy," *Administrative Science Quarterly* 2(March 1958):409-443.

8. Thompson, 1967, ch. 2.

9. See, for example: Paul Lawrence and Jay Lorsch, *Organization and Environment* (Cambridge, Mass.: Harvard University Press, 1967).

10. F.E. Emery and E.L. Trist, "The Causal Texture of Organizational Environment," in *Readings in Organization Theory—A Behavioral Approach*, eds. Walter A. Hill and Douglas Egan (Boston: Allyn and Bacon, 1966): 435-447.

11. Shirley Terreberry, "The Evolution of Organizational Environments," *Administrative Science Quarterly* 12(September 1968):590-613.

12. William M. Evan, "The Organization Set: Toward a Theory of Interorganizational Relations," in *Approaches to Organizational Design*, ed. James D. Thompson (Pittsburgh: University of Pittsburgh Press, 1966): 175-191.

13. Deil S. Wright, "The States and Intergovernmental Relations," *Publius* 1(Winter 1972):7-68.

14. James G. March and Johan P. Olsen, *Ambiguity and Choice in Organizations* (Bergen, Norway: Universitet-Sforlaget, 1976).

15. Richard L. Sutton, "Cultural Context and Change-Agent Organizations," *Administrative Science Quarterly* 19(December 1974):547-562.

16. Herbert A. Simon, *Administrative Behavior*, 3rd ed. (New York: The Free Press, 1976), pp. 48-52.

17; For examples of this approach see: Howard E. Aldrich and Jeffrey Pfeffer, "Environments of Organizations," in *Annual Review of Sociology*, eds. Alex Inkeles, James Coleman, and Neil Smelser Vol. 2 (Palo Alto: Annual Reviews, Inc., 1976): pp. 79-105; Michael Hannan and John H. Freeman, "The Population Ecology of Organizations," in *Environments and Organizations*, ed Marshall W. Meyer (San Francisco: Jossey-Bass Publishers, 1978): pp. 131-171.

18. Hannan and Freeman, 1978, pp. 133-135.

19. Aldrich and Pfeffer, 1976, pp. 80-81.

20. D. Campbell, "Variation and Selective Retention in Socio-cultural Evolution," *General Systems* 16(Summer 1969):69-85.

21. Hannan and Freeman, 1978, p. 143.

22. Eugene Lewis, *American Politics in a Bureaucratic Age* (Cambridge, Mass.: Winthrop Publishers, Inc., 1977), ch. 1.

23. Hannan and Freeman, 1978, pp. 149-150.

24. Aaron Wildavsky, *The Politics of the Budgetary Process*, 3rd ed. (Boston: Little, Brown and Co., 1979).

25. Hannan and Freeman, 1978, p. 141.

26. John Child, "Organizational Structure, Environment and Performance: The Role of Strategic Choice," in *People and Organizations*, eds. Graeme Salaman and Kenneth Thompson (London: The Open University Press, 1973), pp. 1-22.

27. Hannan and Freeman, 1978, p. 132.

28. Stuart M. Schmidt and Thomas A. Kochan, "Interorganizational Relationships: Patterns and Motivations," *Administrative Science Quarterly* 22(June 1977):220-234.

29. Sol Levine and Paul E. White, "Exchange as a Conceptual Framework for the Study of Interorganizational Relationships," *Administrative Science Quarterly* 5(March 1961):583-601.

30. For examples of the power-dependence approach see: J. Kenneth Benson, "The Interorganizational Network as a Political Economy," *Administrative Science Quarterly* 20(June 1975):229-249; Michael Crozier and Jean-Claude Thoenig, "The Regulation of Complex Organized Systems," *Administrative Science Quarterly* 21(December 1976):547-570.

31. Schmidt and Kochan, 1977, pp. 221-223.

32. Jeffrey Pfeffer and Gerald R. Salancik, *The External Control of Organizations* (New York: Harper & Row, 1978), ch. 5.

33. Ibid., ch. 4.

34. Ibid.

35. Burton R. Clark, "Interorganizational Patterns in Education," *Administrative Science Quarterly* 10(September 1965):224-327.

36. Benson, 1975, p. 243.

37. Pfeffer and Salancik, 1978, pp. 44-45.

38. Ibid., p. 51.

39. Hannan and Freeman, 1978, pp. 149-150.

40. George E. Hale and Marion Lief Palley, "Federal Grants to the States: Who Governs?" *Administration and Society* 11(May 1979):3-26.

41. David A. Caputo and Richard L. Cole, *Urban Politics and Decentralization* (Lexington, Mass.: Lexington Books, D.C. Heath and Co., 1974).

42. On the budget maximizing behavior of bureaus and bureaucrats see: Anthony Downs, *Inside Bureaucracy* (Boston: Little, Brown and Co., 1967); William A. Niskanen, Jr., *Bureaucracy and Representative Government* (Chicago: Aldine Publishing Co., 1971).

43. Pfeffer and Salancik, 1978, pp. 106-107.

44. Schmidt and Kochan, 1977, p. 232.

3 Organizations in Criminal Justice

In the last chapter we drew upon theories of interorganizational behavior in proposing a theory of intergovernmental relations and deducing four empirical propositions about federal strategies of influence. This chapter demonstrates that an organizationally based theory is an appropriate choice for the policy area of criminal justice. In the course of this demonstration, the block-grant mechanism will be described in sufficient detail that some substantive understanding will result from the empirical analysis of later chapters.

In contrast to most policy areas, criminal-justice policy has received the attention of very few political scientists. Thus there is neither received wisdom nor longstanding debates on how to study its policy process. As there are no competing theories to consider, it is defensible to concentrate solely on the interorganizational approach described in chapter 2. At this point, though, some plausible reasons for the collective scholarly inattention to criminal justice policy should be considered.

First, perhaps it is the case that crime is not a political issue. The allocation of public resources to fight crime may not be a political process. For a number of reasons, this hardly seems plausible. Citizens see an increase in the crime rate as a public problem, though its relative importance as a issue changes over time. Crime is on the public agenda. Candidates for offices from president to mayor propose programs to fight it. Similarly, there is quite a bit of evidence that the allocation of block-grant funds at the state level is political, though most participants deplore this fact. For example, the attorney general of Alabama testified before Congress that Alabama's SPA was "a politician's dream for the biggest pork barrel of them all."[1] A judge from another state told Congress that

> Already there is tough competition between all elements of the LEAA program at a State level. There is backscratching; there is logrolling. All sorts of such activity will continue with increased intensity so that other elements of the criminal justice system can keep and continue their programs that are in existence at this time. . . . Courts should never get into the arena of competition or into the pit of competition and have to fight other elements for funds. Whenever courts get into a pit of competition, inevitably an atmosphere is created which is conducive to political influence. This would be abhorrent to think about.[2]

At the national level it has been alleged that certain discretionary programs of LEAA have been political footballs, particularly under President Nixon.[3]

There may be some truth to such contentions. The interviews we conducted revealed that some participants still believe Nixon pressured mayors to lower crime rates just before elections. It is likely that, within the criminal-justice area, allocations of resources are determined by factors of interest to political scientists. These political factors are not likely to be partisan or electoral in nature. Both political parties agree that crime is an important problem and both are against it. One explanation for the dearth of political-science studies on this topic is the narrow definition of politics held by the profession rather than the absence of politics in the allocation process.

A second explanation of the inattention to criminal-justice policy is the nature of the funds supporting this policy. Scholars studying comparative state politics might have avoided this area due to lack of state discretion under federal funding. If there is no state-to-state variation in policy outputs, the policy area would be intrinsically uninteresting to students of state politics. This reason for avoiding the study of the criminal-justice process is unfounded. Under the block-grant arrangement, states have considerable discretion to formulate and implement policies. Categorical grants-in-aid are dedicated to specific purposes, but block-grant funds can be spent in a variety of ways to fight crime. Such federal funds must be spent in accordance with a state plan that guarantees that allocative decisions are made consciously and not randomly. There is probably considerable variation from one state to another in funding priorities.

A third reason for avoiding the study of criminal-justice politics is a sense of the impending demise of the most prominent federal actor in this policy area. LEAA's possible abolition was frequently used as an argument against undertaking this book in the fall of 1977. The defense is that political scientists ought to study failures as well as successes. Indeed, policy termination should be as important as policy initiation on the scholarly agenda.

Organizational Dominance in Criminal Justice

The organizational elements of the adult criminal justice system are described here—police, courts, and corrections. Following the scheme of Salisbury and Heinz, this system's policy process is conceptualized as consisting of two stages: structural and allocative.[4] The *structural stage* occurs at the national level, primarily in Congress, where the structures or rules for the block grant's allocation are set up. At this level the chief activity of individual organizations is to acquire resources for the entire criminal-justice organizational system and set up rules for their future allocation which advantage the individual organizations. The *allocative stage* occurs at the state level where SPAs subgrant their state's block-grant funds to projects. The chief organizational activity at this level is to acquire resources for one's own organization. At both stages the federal and state governments attempt to influence participating organizations, following the exchange and power-dependency strategies.

Our research had several components: reading transcripts from all the authorization hearings in the Senate and House; attending congressional hearings during 1977 and 1978; reading governmental and scholarly reports of LEAA; examining the flow of LEAA funds to criminal-justice organizations; and interviewing representatives of nine of the most active interest groups involved at the national level. The identities of individuals interviewed cannot be revealed. However, the groups included one from each criminal-justice function and one from each governmental jurisdiction receiving block-grant funds. The interviews were conducted by the authors in Washington and Chicago during June 1978. Members of Congress, their staff members, officials of LEAA, or SPA employees were not interviewed. A different description might have emerged from extensive interviewing of all the participants, but limited resources did not permit it. The interviewing was intended to supplement the principal form of empirical analysis, which was statistical analysis of project data at the state level. This supplementary, qualitative research provided insights about organizations' roles that could not be derived from quantitative data analysis.

Components of the Criminal-Justice System

The adult criminal-justice system consists of three major functional components: police, corrections, and courts (which includes prosecution and defense). The juvenile component is not considered for several reasons. First, its personnel are not so clearly organized into three functions but are more oriented to the particular age group they are serving. Second, until 1974, the Department of Health, Education and Welfare (HEW) had authority over juvenile lawbreakers. At that time, the Juvenile Justice and Delinquency Prevention Act transferred authority to LEAA, and additional monies in the block grant were earmarked for juveniles. Since juvenile crime is a relative newcomer to the block-grant program, it was excluded from this book.

The total expenditure for criminal-justice purposes by all governments in the fiscal year (FY) 1976 was nearly $20 billion, making it the fifth largest domestic function of government.[5] Local governments (cities and counties) spent 61 percent of this total; state governments, 26 percent; federal government, 13 percent. When these totals are broken down by function, 48.7 percent of the resources is spent on police protection; 14.2 percent is spent on judicial, public defense, and legal services; and 8.6 percent is spent on corrections.[6] If a function's political strength is related to its funding, these figures give a preliminary indication of the relative political strength of each functional component. Since the police receive such a high proportion of the resources, it is expected that they are greatly advantaged in the political arena relative to courts and corrections.

In terms of employment, over 1 million persons were involved on a full-time basis in criminal-justice activities. Relative political strength may also be reflected in each function's employment figures. On the basis of personnel, there is even more evidence of the police advantage: police employees constitute 71.7 percent of all criminal-justice employees; courts, 15.8 percent; and corrections, 11.8 percent. This nationwide perspective suggests that the nation's 625,000 to 700,000 police officers will be important in influencing criminal-justice policy, just in terms of sheer numbers. The relative advantage of the police may vary from state to state since the proportion of the total employed by each function varies. Also their advantage differs according to governmental level since the functions tend to concentrate at different levels. Police and, to a lesser extent, courts personnel are predominantly employed at the local level, and corrections personnel, mostly at the state level.

The nation's police officers are distributed among some 20,000 separate police forces but a majority of them are concentrated in large municipal police forces. The chief reform proposal has been to consolidate these smaller forces (90 percent of the 20,000 forces have less than ten officers) into larger units serving a metropolitan or regional area. Already most city police officers are unionized and this trend should continue as police forces are combined. In a recent survey of cities, 64 percent of cities reported that their police were covered by formal collective bargaining agreements, and 36 percent by informal agreements.[7] Nearly half of the cities report that local associations represent their officers, with Fraternal Order of Police and American Federation of State, County, and Municipal Employees also representing significant numbers of city police forces.[8] Unionization has brought higher salaries and more benefits (such as pensions) to police officers. It also contributes greatly to their clout within the criminal-justice system. The state and county police and sheriffs tend not to be unionized. Unfortunately, unionization data are not available on a state-by-state basis so a more indirect measure of clout must be used.

In addition to their union activities, the police also have very active professional associations that lobby on their behalf in Washington. The largest of these groups is the International Association of Chiefs of Police (IACP). It has around 12,000 members in 64 countries, a staff of 112, and an annual budget of about $5 million. Other associations in the police area that have been involved in LEAA legislation include the National Association of State Directors of Law Enforcement Training, National Association of Police Community Relations Officers, Police Foundation, National Sheriffs Association, and National Black Police Association.

The courts component of the criminal-justice system employs about 160,000 persons who perform three separate and distinct tasks: prosecution, defense, and judgment. In each of these task areas, important reforms are taking place that encourage centralization. Prosecution has typically been a part-time job at the county level, but the move is toward a centrally supervised full-time profession. The delivery of indigent defense services at the county level is rapidly changing from assigned counsel to full-time salaried defenders. Similarly, there is substantial movement toward placing the nation's 15,000 separate courts under a unified, state-supervised system.

Though the courts component is fragmented by task orientation, it is unified by and derives its political clout from the fact that most of its members share a common profession—the law. The courts sector's interest in LEAA legislation is articulated by a number of professional associations. The largest of these is the American Bar Association with 230,000 members, a staff of over 500, and an annual budget of about $22 million. Other courts groups active in Washington are the National Association for Court Administration, National District Attorney's Association (NDAA), National Association of Attorneys General, National Center for State Courts, Lawyers' Committee for Civil Rights Under Law, National Legal Aid and Defender Association, National Council of Juvenile Court Judges, National Association of Pre-trial Service Agencies, American Judicature Society, Conference of Chief Justices, Conference of State Court Administrators, National American Indian Court Judges Association, National Association of Trial Court Administrators, and National Conference of Appellate Courts Clerks.

The 120,000 persons employed in correctional services constitute the weakest of the three components in terms of political clout. They have neither the large numbers of the police nor the high prestige of these with legal degrees. The active interest groups are fewer in number: American Correctional Association (ACA), National Association of State Drug Abuse Program Coordinators, Association of State Correctional Institutions, and National Association of Juvenile Delinquency Program Administrators. The largest group is the American Correctional Association with 12,000 members, a budget of around $5 million, and a staff of fourteen. Unlike the other two functional components, a majority of corrections personnel are employed at the state level, though county and city services are also numerous. Rather than centralization, the primary drive for reform is toward the integration of separate services such as probation, parole, jails, and prisons.

Structural Policy

A *structural policy* is a policy that establishes authoritative rules to guide future allocation of resources. An example is the legislature's creation of a higher-education board to allocate money to state colleges instead of allocating money separately to each college. A structural policy is different from an *allocative policy* (for example, an expenditure), which allocates tangible benefits directly to persons or groups. The original legislation that sets up a block-grant program and Congress' subsequent amendments are structural policies because they set up a formula by which federal money is allocated to states and some criteria by which states allocate the money thereafter. In a block-grant program, structural-policy action is set at the national level whereas allocation takes place at the state level.

The Omnibus Crime Control and Safe Streets Act. In the 1964 presidential campaign, candidates Barry Goldwater and Lyndon Johnson both identified crime as a national problem. After his election, President Johnson established the President's Commission on Law Enforcement and Administration of Justice. Its report clearly identified inertia on the part of the three criminal-justice functions as a major problem for federal attention:

> Many of the criminal justice system's difficulties stem from its reluc-
> tance to change old ways or, to put the same proposition in reverse,
> its reluctance to try new ones. The increasing volume of crime in
> America establishes conclusively that many of the old ways are not
> good enough. Innovation and experimentation in all parts of the
> criminal justice system are clearly imperative. They are imperative with
> respect to entire agencies and to specific procedures. . . . The Commis-
> sion believes that the first step toward improvement is for officials in
> all parts of the system to face their problems?[9]

President Johnson next proposed legislation for a pilot program of federal grants in the criminal-justice area. This bill, creating the Office of Law Enforcement Assistance, was passed with little or no opposition in Congress even though organizations representing both police chiefs and judges were said to be opposed to "federal encroachment" in the law-enforcement field.[10] Thus criminal-justice organizations tried to stop the forerunner of the grant program, though without success. Presumably these organizations preferred the status quo, in which state and local governments had the governing authority, to an unknown situation where the federal government had control.

The Crime Control and Safe Streets Act was proposed by President Johnson in his State of the Union address of January 1967 and contained nearly all of the major recommendations of the earlier presidential commission on crime. The program Johnson proposed, however, bore little resemblance to the bill passed by Congress. The president had proposed direct categorical grants to communities, a strategy consistent with his "direct federalism" approach to urban problems. The idea of a block grant was suggested by the House Republi-can leadership, Everett Dirksen and Gerald Ford. They argued that state govern-ments could allocate federal money more efficiently and responsibly than could the federal government. Additionally, Dirksen is supposed to have said that he was "not about to see (Attorney General) Ramsey Clark handle $500 mil-lion."[11]

The block-grant idea was also supported by most of the nation's governors, partly due to their fear that federal control of the police would result from a categorical program. In addition to the governors, the state legislators and county representatives also lobbied for the block-grant concept. An analysis of governors' letters to Congress regarding the proposed legislation shows that Alabama and Wyoming were the only states to remain in opposition to the bill after the block-grant concept was incorporated into the bill.[12] The writer from Alabama said:

> We cannot comprehend any great material benefit from this proposed legislation, however noble its purpose or intent. The Passage of this act and application of its proposals in our opinion would make very little, if any, dent in the crime statistics in this nation. . . . It has been our observation in other areas of Federal Grants to the states, that with the giving of the money comes the strife of intervention and with federal authorities in their apparent desire to control, come the mountain of red tape, inspection, rules and regulations, guidelines. etc.[13]

Opposition to the block grant came from representatives of the cities (such as the National League of Cities) and the mayors, and from Northern Democrats in the Congress. They preferred a direct federal-local categorical program, which would retain control at the local level, rather than the transfer of power to the state level, which the block grant would entail. When funds flow to cities through the state government, city officials fear that their share of the funds will be smaller than if the funds flow directly to the cities.

It is interesting that the idea for a national program to fight crime was a presidential initiative, not the initiative of the groups to be benefited. Initial debate over federal-funding strategies attracted the attention of the public interest groups not of the criminal-justice groups. Criminal-justice groups were more interested in the provisions of the legislation directed at gun control, wire-tapping, and rights of criminal defendants. Most of their congressional testimony was on those titles and not the block grant.

The events of 1967 and 1968—riots in Detroit, Newark, and other cities and the assassination of Martin Luther King, Jr.,—eventually turned nearly all attention away from the block-grant and toward the gun-control issue. Consequently, the later congressional hearings focused primarily on the latter titles. On the day of Robert Kennedy's assassination, the Omnibus Crime Control and Safe Streets Act passed Congress. It was signed into law on 20 June 1968.

The chief goal of the act was for the national government to help state and local governments to achieve their own goals of preventing and controlling crime:

> Congress finds that the high incidence of crime in the United States threatens the peace, security, and general welfare of the Nation and its

citizens. To prevent crime and to insure the greater safety of the people, law enforcement efforts must be better coordinated, intensified, and made more effective at all levels of government.

Congress finds further that crime is essentially a local problem that must be dealt with by State and local governments if it is to be controlled effectively.

It is therefore the declared policy of the Congress to assist State and local governments in strengthening and improving law enforcement at every level by national assistance.[14]

To achieve this goal, Congress created the Law Enforcement Assistance Administration. It is authorized to make three types of grants—planning, training and research, and action grants. The training and research funds are administered at the national level, while planning funds and 85 percent of the action funds are allocated in block grants to states (calculated on the basis of population). The remaining 15 percent of the action funds are discretionary funds to be distributed at the national level by LEAA. Planning monies cover 90 percent of the cost of the operation of SPAs created by each state's governor. Action funds are allocated by the SPAs to state and local units of government. Matching funds of 25 to 50 percent, depending on the purpose, are provided by the state. Action funds can be spent for a variety of purposes, though prevention and control of riots and organized crime were initially given special emphasis. The law also specified that a considerable amount of money has to be actually spent at the local level: 40 percent of the planning funds and 75 percent of the action funds.

The purposes of the SPAs are to develop a comprehensive statewide plan for fighting crime, to incorporate innovations and advanced techniques into the projects they fund, to establish priorities for the improvement of law enforcement, and to coordinate programs and projects on a statewide basis. LEAA action funds can be spent by a SPA only after LEAA approval of its plan. The plan has to include descriptions of existing resources, needs, problems, priorities, and a plan for coordination, as well as provisions for balance between state and local units of government. Instances of nonapproval of a plan are rare. Indeed the only time LEAA has rejected a state's plan and withheld money was from the District of Columbia in 1977.

The original legislation had some attractive features for a variety of groups: the states, cities, and police. The block-grant feature gave states some power in an area previously dominated by local governments. The National Association of Counties, National Governors' Association, and the National Conference of State Legislatures claimed the acceptance of the block-grant concept as a victory.[15] Yet, the provision that 75 percent of action funds has to be spent locally was a victory for the cities. The emphasis on riots and organized crime favored the police over the other two functional components.

The Crime Control and Safe Streets Act has been modified by Congress four times since 1968. A brief review of each reauthorization period presents the conflicts among competing interests.

1970 Amendments. The first reauthorization hearings were held in 1970. Battle lines were drawn among functional components of criminal justice (police, courts, and corrections) and between state and local governmental levels. The congressional compromise, as enacted in the Omnibus Crime Control Act of 1970, retained the block-grant concept and hence favored the governors over the mayors. The mayors lost further ground when states were no longer required to pass on a certain percentage of planning funds to local units. If LEAA deemed the "pass through" requirement inappropriate, SPAs could retain the planning funds. The new law did require, however, that state plans allocate "an adequate share" of action funds to areas with high crime rates or with high law-enforcement activity. This was a minor victory for the cities. Their second victory was the creation of local criminal-justice coordinating councils, which were authorized to do the planning for large cities. Additionally, the reduction of the required state and local matching funds to 25 percent was a boon to both states and cities.

Congress reduced the favored position of the police, who had been the recipients of a large proportion of SPA subgrants from Title C funds. A *categorization* or earmarking amendment set up Part E action funds exclusively for corrections, authorizing $120 million nationally for that purpose. This was the first time monies were set aside specifically for one functional component. Also the amendment stipulated that SPAs could not reduce their previous level of correctional funding from Part C action funds. Hence, total corrections expenditures could only increase. Within Part E, half of the funds were discretionary (disbursed by LEAA) and half went to states on a formula basis to be subgranted by SPAs. Interestingly enough, the earmarking of monies for corrections seems to have been the idea of LEAA officials rather than corrections officials.[16]

1973 Amendments. In the 1973 round of reauthorization hearings, the status quo was maintained, though the mayors made their usual attempt to change the block-grant program into direct grants to cities. A more serious assault on the block-grant concept was President Nixon's proposal to convert LEAA into a special revenue-sharing program more in line with his New Federalism philosophy. This shift would have involved dropping requirements such as matching funds and federal approval of the states' plans. The atmosphere was further charged by a scathing report issued by the Democratic majority of the Monagan committee in 1972. It called the LEAA program inefficient, wasteful, maladministered, and in some cases corrupt.[17] For the first time there was an attempt made in Congress to kill LEAA entirely rather than to reauthorize it.

Amidst this criticism LEAA survived with only a few changes in its basic program. The most important changes in the program were a further lowering of the match requirement to 90/10 on most projects, and an enlarging of the explicit mandate of the program to include all criminal-justice activities, rather than just law enforcement. A new provision favoring the cities allowed the larger local jurisdictions to submit a single comprehensive plan for SPA approval rather than individual project proposals. Otherwise, the organizational system of functional and jurisdictional interests fought off criticism and major change.

1976 Amendments. In 1976, the next round of reauthorization hearings occurred amidst calls for a fundamental rethinking of the agency due to the continued criticism voiced by some interest groups, Congress, and the public. Again the struggle among state, city, and county representatives for more control was essentially a standoff. State legislators succeeded in gaining more influence in the process. Rather than governors, state legislators were authorized to create SPAs and to review their state plans, though without a veto. The new emphasis in 1976 favorable to local governments was the community anticrime programs, whereby a separate program with earmarked funds was set up to respond to citizens' groups applying for grant funds. Despite these minor changes, the federal-state-local balance was essentially undisturbed.

The resolution of the interfunctional rivalries was increased funding for courts and guaranteed representation for the courts sector on SPA advisory boards. The functional balance further changed with the elimination of the emphasis on riot control within law enforcement. This implicitly gave lower priority to the police function. The final addition to the program, evaluation requirements, presumably reflected the continued criticism of the program and in particular its failure to reduce the nation's crime rate.

The Organizational Network

In describing briefly the outcome of each congressional reauthorization, it is obvious that groups other than those representing police, the courts, and corrections are important. Equally active and important are the groups representing interests of the various governmental jurisdictions that receive or desire to receive LEAA funds.

Active Groups. The active jurisdictional or public interest groups include National Governors' Association (NGA), National Conference of State Legislatures (NCSL), National Association of Counties (NACO), National League of Cities (NLC), U.S. Conference of Mayors, National Association of Regional Councils, Education Commission of the States, National Conference of Commissions on Uniform State Laws, International City Management Association, and Council of State Governments. The major groups (NGA, NCSL, NACO and NLC) all have at least one staff person assigned to lobby Congress on criminal-justice matters. NLC and NACO are the largest of these groups. NLC has a staff of 110 (6 of whom are assigned to criminal-justice matters) and an annual budget of $5 million. NACO has the same size staff and a budget of $4 million yearly. NCSL employs around 75 people on its budget of $2 million to $3 million, while NGA has roughly 63 employees and a budget of $1 million.

The public interest groups, particularly NACO, NGA, NCSL, and NLC, have testified more often than have criminal-justice groups such as the American Bar Association, American Correctional Association, National District Attorneys' Association, and International Association of Chiefs of Police. The chief point of the congressional presentations of the public-interest groups usually is that their bailiwicks should get more money. In fact, they may be more self-interested than the functional groups, who at least said that their function should not get all the funds. One interviewee said that members of Congress do not regard criminal-justice groups' testimony to be as legitimate as that of the public-interest groups because their jobs and professions are at stake.[18] LEAA dollars benefit the governmental jurisdictions just as much as the criminal-justice professions. Dependencies on the federal government are created for both groups. Within the public-interest sector, the groups meet twice a year to discuss LEAA. Representatives of states (governors, state legislators, and SPA directors) tend to talk to one another, and representatives of localities (cities and counties) to one another, although there are some examples of state-local coalitions.

Involvement by the private sector is secured through citizens' groups which are sporadically active on criminal-justice issues: National Council of Jewish Women, General Federation of Women's Clubs, National Congress of American Indians, Association for Children with Learning Disabilities, National Assembly of Voluntary Health and Welfare Organizations, Associations of Junior Leagues, National Conference of Christians and Jews, National Board of Young Men's Christian Associations, Center for Women's Policy Studies, National Council of Senior Citizens, National Council of Negro Women, American Medical Association, Council on Population and Environment, American Public Welfare Association, American Management Association, American Association of Retired Persons, National Retired Teachers Association, National Tribal Chairmen's Association, National Urban Coalition, Committee for Economic Development, American Civil Liberties Union, Friends (Quakers) Committee on National Legislation, National Urban League, and American Jewish Committee. Each of these groups is active episodically on matters that affect its membership, but in general they are not as active as the groups previously mentioned. Hence, none of these groups were interviewed.

In addition, there are some groups that purport to represent the entire criminal-justice system: National Council on Crime and Delinquency, National Association of Citizens Crime Commissions, Americans United Against Crime, and National Conference of State Criminal Justice Planning Administrators. The SPA Conference is somewhat different from the others as it represents directly the director of the SPAs. All of the state directors are members of this organization and they are served by nine staff members. The SPA Conference is a very strong defender of the block-grant concept and it attempts to halt *creeping categorization* or earmarking of block-grant funds. At the same time, it opposes any trend toward special revenue sharing. The SPA directors would no longer be needed under such a funding strategy.[19]

Lobbying Tactics. The common goal of all the groups already mentioned could be characterized as resource acquisition. They want to get more money for criminal justice, and LEAA is the federal program that provides money for this purpose. When reauthorization and appropriations decisions are made in Congress, all the groups try to make a good case for the continuance of the program and its increased financing. At the same time, each group wants to expand its own share of criminal-justice resources. Each group presents a positive evaluation of accomplishments in its own sector and, at least by implication, a less positive evaluation of the accomplishments of others. They lobby Congress and LEAA trying to structure the program so that their own share is expanded.

Of the nine groups interviewed, most had testified at least once at a congressional hearing. Regardless of the frequency with which the groups testified, all reported that they were satisfied with their access to Congress, though they were not always pleased with their impact on the outcome. One very prestigious group of criminal-justice professionals said, "Testimony is not necessary. We only testify if it is necessary. Whenever possible we use an easier route, like conversation."[20] This group also reported that it has input into policy formulation prior to hearings. All groups reported engaging in formal discussions of legislation with key members of Congress and subcommittee staff members.

All groups interviewed report extensive, almost daily, contact with top LEAA administrators. "We are always being invited to conferences and workshops. LEAA officials are there. They pick up our ideas and use them."[21] The groups report that LEAA and administration officials listen and usually grant some of what they want. Only one group, representing a criminal-justice profession, said it was "written off" by LEAA.[22]

Another technique used by these groups is to mobilize their grass-roots constituencies to acquire more resources from Congress. None of the functional groups, however, thought that they were particularly successful in mobilizing their members. One director sends monthly intelligence reports to his membership. He sometimes asks them to take action but rarely with much success. Another group mobilizes its state and local associations if the issue is important enough. Its national organization passed a resolution urging its state and local associations to become more involved with SPAs, but the state and local associations lack sufficient staff for extended participation. Two of the public-interest groups reported attempts to mobilize individual elected officials for letter-writing campaigns.

Overall, the conclusion is that the public-interest groups are somewhat more sophisticated in their lobbying techniques than are the functional groups. Representatives of criminal-justice groups did not talk about coalition building or other strategic matters, whereas the public-interest groups mentioned specific coalitional victories. Within the criminal-justice sector, professional groups tend not to talk to each other, although sometimes they do talk with the public-interest groups. When the executive director of one of the criminal-justice groups was asked if he ever talked with other criminal-justice groups, he said, "That's a good idea. We ought to do that. Maybe we would be stronger together."[23] In contrast, the public-interest groups interact regularly.

These interest groups tend to underestimate their influence at the federal level. One authority on the police and political organizations, James Q. Wilson, believes that the functional organizations (criminal-justice syndicals) are the major barriers to effective change and constitute serious impediments to the federal government's progress.[24]

Federal Strategies of Influence in the Organizational Network

A focus on exchange and power dependency as federal strategies explains much about the achievement of federal goals in an intergovernmental system. These two strategies work at the national level through the federal government, which tries to influence the active organizations, at the same time that these organizations are lobbying Congress and LEAA.

The Power-Dependency Strategy. LEAA tries to make organizations dependent on it for resources so that it can gain power over them. By manipulating resource flow, LEAA can influence the actions of the target organization. LEAA grants discretionary money to each of the nine groups that were interviewed and to many other groups. Some of it is for special projects that allow the hiring of additional short-term staff. Some LEAA money, however, is for long-term funding of core staff involved in dissemination of information about LEAA and membership services. The groups reported with some pride how they communicate LEAA developments to their membership. Some grants are made to the research section of an organization, whereas others are made to the lobbying section of the organization. The figures, presented in table 3-1, do not distinguish between the two types of grants. They do indicate that, given the size of the annual budgets of the organizations, LEAA's financial support in whatever form is important to these organizations' survival. One cannot expect that these organizations will be too critical of the agency that is so important to their maintenance and growth.

Table 3-1
Total LEAA Grants (Nonblock) to National Organizations,
1974 to 1977

Public-interest groups	$ 4,699,937
Criminal-justice groups	46,800,555
Police	8,147,489
Courts	27,320,615
Corrections	3,920,808
Cross system	7,411,643
Other groups	14,260,900
Total	65,761,392

Source: Calculated by authors from data in PROFILE system.

The SPA Conference seems to be the group that is most dependent on LEAA. It would not exist apart from the block-grant program, whereas the public-interest and functional groups would continue by virtue of support from state and local governments. The SPA Conference, in particular, views information dissemination as one of its main tasks. If LEAA officials need to reach SPA directors fast or informally, the SPA Conference arranges meetings so that federal officials can meet their constituents. The SPA Conference views itself as a central external clearance point for LEAA guidelines. It circulates guidelines to state directors, gathers their comments, and returns them to LEAA. Also, it is sometimes involved in policy development prior to the issuance of guidelines.

Exchange Strategy. The second federal strategy, the exchange strategy, is also evident at the national level. By controlling the decisional premises of criminal-justice personnel, LEAA can influence their actions. In large part, exchange is accomplished through encouraging professionalism on the part of criminal-justice practitioners and planners. Professionals share a wide variety of values and beliefs. State, local, and federal professionals are assumed to be likely to agree on desirable policy goals. LEAA itself has spent $374 million for training programs and has stimulated SPAs to fund similar programs. Under the Law Enforcement Education Program (LEEP), practitioners (police officers, courts and corrections personnel) have received financial assistance for college study, amounting to $350 million. This program was paised highly by the groups interviewed.

LEAA has also furnished the functional associations with funds for *stand-ards-and-goals projects,* that is, each function has developed standards of professionalism and of conduct, as well as for the physical condition of equipment and buildings in which their clientele resides. Then each national association attempts to implement these standards at the state and local level. These projects were viewed as very significant improvements by the groups that were interviewed.

At the same time LEAA has been trying to raise the professionalism of existing personnel, it has also been trying to create an entirely new profession, criminal-justice planning. Planners are to think in long-range terms and in systems terms, in contrast to the partial perspectives of practitioners. Funds amounting to $25 million have been provided to universities to begin criminal-justice graduate programs. The products of these new programs are more likely to share the norms and values of LEAA professionals than are practitioners, even newly-trained ones. In addition to shared values, these criminal-justice professionals are bound to LEAA by dependence. They are dependent (for jobs) on the survival of the block-grant program which requires planning, whereas the demand for practitioners in each function continues no matter what happens to LEAA.

The dependency and exchange strategies are attempted at the national level. Later chapters will report their effect: Are federal policy directives followed more closely as a result of these strategies? LEAA is trying to influence organizations while those same organizations are lobbying LEAA and the Congress. One situation where the outcome of this organizational interaction can be seen is in the 1979 reauthorization process in Congress, which nearly resulted in the abolition of LEAA.

1979 Amendments

During the 1976 presidential campaign, candidate Jimmy Carter often criticized LEAA and promised to restructure it if he were elected. As president, Carter did not appoint a permanent administrator of the agency, pending a full-scale review of its operations. Instead, he appointed a task force in the Justice Department to conduct a review. In August of 1977 the task force submitted a report that called for abolition of LEAA. Another year passed while the Carter administration studied the report and drafted a reauthorization bill in consultation with Senator Edward Kennedy, now chairman of the Senate Judiciary Committee.

In July of 1978 President Carter announced details of the Justice System Improvement Act, which was introduced by Senator Kennedy on July 10, 1978. Though Carter asserted that the bill would solve the many problems he had previously identified, it definitely was not an abolition bill.[25] At most it was a reorganization bill. The final version cleared Congress on 13 December 1979.

The fundamental principle of the block grant to states remains intact, with 80 percent of the funds being distributed on a block-grant basis to states for reallocation. There are now two block-grant formulas: one based strictly on population; another based on population, crime rate, criminal-justice expenditures, and tax effort. The state can choose whichever formula is most beneficial to it, as in revenue sharing. States must still apply for funds as they are not automatically disbursed. A desire to control states' purchases resulted in a requirement of substantive approval of funding requests by the federal government. Carter wanted to place strict limitations on the purchase of equipment and hardware, primarily to eliminate the purchase of Buck Rogers-type police gadgets.[26]

The program was not converted into a special revenue-sharing program for criminal justice as promised earlier. Congressman John Conyers charged that most of the money will still go to the same receipients, for the same purposes.[27]

There are still strings attached. Some state and local matching (10 percent) remains in the formula-grant program. One maintenance-of-effort provision remains, focusing on juvenile delinquency. SPAs will be renamed Criminal Justice Councils but they will still analyze criminal-justice problems, establish priorities for expenditure of funds based on the analysis, approve and disapprove applications from other units for the federal funds, and submit applications for funds. States will file applications only every third year instead of annually, with eight rather than twenty-four required items in the applications. Carter's choice was the reduction of the amount of red tape rather than the abolition of the program. The cities gained a victory: states must grant a fixed allocation (*mini-block grant*) to cities with more than 100,000 population. States now have much less authority to disapprove the applications of these larger cities.[28]

LEAA itself is joined by a new and equal Office of Justice Assistance, Research, and Statistics (OJARS). Together they are authorized to spend $1 billion, a substantial increase over the 1979 LEAA appropriation of $648 million. However, only $486 million was appropriated by the Congress for FY 1980, though Senator Kennedy pushed the Senate and the president for a larger appropriation.

One final and very interesting feature of the bill is that the goals of the act are considerably scaled down from the original ones of controlling crime and making the streets safe. The 1979 bill is entitled the "Justice System Improvement Act" and it mentions combating crime—not reducing, controlling, or preventing it. Clearly, it will be easier to make progress toward the goals of combating crime and improving the system than it was to achieve the goal of reducing crime. This is a significant retreat from a measurable goal for which an agency could be held accountable.

What does the passage of this legislation tell us about the structural-policy process? LEAA was roundly criticized by everyone from President Carter to the person in the street. It was not protected by its department head, Attorney General Griffin Bell, who opposed LEAA even more than Carter did. It was not protected by its agency head, since Carter never appointed one. Yet the agency survived.

The strength of the organizational system (including LEAA) is the only explanation for LEAA's survival. The two years of uncertainty while Carter made up his mind about the agency allowed the criminal-justice constituency plenty of time to mobilize. In particular, allowing the task force to recommend abolition was "very naive; the White House blew it," according to one interest-group source.[29] This announcement sent the system into action to preserve its resource base.

The Allocational-Policy Process

Block-grant funds of two types—planning and action—are given to states on a population-formula basis. Planning funds support the activities of the SPAs, regional planning units (RPUs), and the criminal-justice coordinating councils (CJCCs), which are the planning units for large cities. The SPAs decide what sorts of projects are needed to deal with their states' crime problems and draw up plans for spending action funds in line with their goals. Then SPAs receive grant proposals from governmental units and private organizations. They award (or subgrant) action funds to proposed projects that are congruent with their plan for the state. Organizations seeking to maximize their share of resources submit grant proposals on topics mentioned in the plan.

SPAs were initially staff agencies designated by governors but now they are statutorily created by the legislature. The governor appoints the advisory board and the SPA director who in turn hires the agency staff which is part of the state civil service or merit system. The relative amount of influence of the board and the staff varies from one state to another. In twenty-two states, the board accepts staff recommendations with review; in twenty-one states, the board reviews and approves specific activities; in twenty-one states, the board's review is more general.[30] Potential recipients are interested in the composition of both bodies and are particularly interested in obtaining representation on them.

Advisory Boards. The SPA advisory boards of different states vary in their composition and size (from eight to seventy-five, averaging twenty-six). The Safe Streets Act (as amended) requires balanced representation among eight different categories, including state and local officials, representatives of each criminal-justice functional sector, citizens, and urban-rural constituencies. The Advisory Commission on Intergovernmental Relations (ACIR) has noted a trend to more representation from the general public and somewhat less from the police sector.[31]

The analysis of 1976 representation, given in table 3-2, shows a somewhat different trend, though it may be partially due to the method of counting. The calculations are not quite comparable to ACIR's. We included any member of the legal profession (other than elected officials) as a representative of the courts sector, that is, lawyers were not deemed to represent the general public.

Table 3-2
Representation on SPA Supervisory Boards, 1976

State	% Law Enforcement	% Corrections	% Courts	% General Government	% Citizens
Alabama	22.9	8.3	27.1	20.8	20.8
Alaska	18.2	9.1	36.4	18.2	18.2
Arizona	13.6	13.6	27.3	36.4	9.1
Arkansas	30.0	20.0	25.0	20.0	5.0
California	11.5	11.5	34.6	23.1	19.2
Colorado	24.0	4.0	32.0	36.0	4.0
Connecticut	28.6	14.3	28.6	19.0	9.5
Delaware	18.8	6.3	25.0	31.3	18.8
Florida	19.4	19.4	22.6	32.3	6.5
Georgia	21.6	8.1	21.6	27.0	21.6
Hawaii	20.0	6.7	26.7	33.3	13.3
Idaho	22.2	3.7	25.9	40.7	7.4
Illinois	28.0	0	28.0	12.0	32.0
Indiana	15.0	10.0	25.0	35.0	15.0
Iowa	22.2	22.2	22.2	0	33.3
Kansas	17.6	5.9	29.4	41.2	5.9
Kentucky	13.2	9.4	37.7	18.9	20.8
Louisiana	38.8	3.0	31.3	11.9	14.9
Maine	30.0	5.0	20.0	15.0	30.0
Maryland	6.9	10.3	41.4	34.5	6.9
Massachusetts	17.1	12.2	43.9	14.6	12.2
Michigan	17.1	8.6	28.6	37.1	8.6
Minnesota	26.9	15.4	26.9	15.4	15.4
Mississippi	23.1	7.7	26.9	23.1	19.2
Missouri	17.6	17.6	41.2	5.9	17.6
Montana	18.8	12.5	25.0	25.0	18.8
Nebraska	22.7	4.5	27.3	22.7	22.7
Nevada	29.4	17.6	35.3	11.8	5.9
New Hampshire	26.7	10.0	13.3	6.7	43.3
New Jersey	22.7	4.5	18.2	31.8	22.7
New Mexico	11.8	5.9	29.4	35.3	17.6
New York	15.4	11.5	19.2	30.8	23.1
North Carolina	21.4	7.1	21.4	42.9	7.1
North Dakota	21.2	15.2	18.2	33.3	12.1
Ohio	19.0	4.8	23.8	33.3	19.0
Oklahoma	23.1	2.6	38.5	10.3	25.6
Oregon	15.8	5.3	21.1	36.8	21.1
Pennsylvania	12.5	6.3	12.5	43.8	25.0
Rhode Island	26.9	3.8	26.9	19.2	23.1
South Carolina	27.3	9.1	18.2	18.2	27.3
South Dakota	11.1	5.6	33.3	38.9	11.1
Tennessee	17.1	9.8	24.4	26.8	22.0
Texas	16.0	4.0	48.0	8.0	24.0
Utah	15.4	3.8	19.2	50.0	11.5
Vermont	15.0	5.0	35.0	20.0	25.0
Virginia	15.0	15.0	35.0	25.0	10.0
Washington	20.7	0	17.2	37.9	24.1
West Virginia	21.2	24.2	12.1	27.3	15.2
Wisconsin	13.3	3.3	33.3	30.0	20.0
Wyoming	28.0	8.0	28.0	4.0	32.0

Source: Calculated by authors from 1977 Planning Documents.

In nearly half the states (23.5 percent), general government (state and local officials such as mayors and state legislators) had the most representation on the board. In seventeen states the courts sector had the most representatives, and this was prior to the recent change in the statute that guaranteed them representation. By 1976 law enforcement was prominent in only a few states. Corrections clearly had the least representation: in only three states did it have even 20 percent of the members. Across all advisory boards, by 1976 the courts sector led with an average of 27.4 percent of the seats, law enforcement was second with 20.2 percent and corrections was a poor third with 9.0 percent. Apparently, corrections lacks political clout at the state level as well as the national level.

In the allocation phase, it would seem that the courts sector would be advantaged in the competition for funds by its access to SPA decisionmakers, corrections would be disadvantaged, and police would rank somewhere between these two. Of course, states vary; the balance among the three functions might be greatly affected by the affiliation of the general government representatives. If they represent state government, then corrections (predominantly a state function) might be more favored by the board.

SPA Staff. Organizations seeking to maximize their resources might attempt to gain access to the staff rather than the board. The conventional wisdom is that staffs are more powerful than boards. The SPA staff writes the plan, recommends funding of grants, and administers them. Thus the staff is important in determining allocation of action funds—who gets what, when, and how. It is therefore important to examine staffs' compositions as a measure of functions' organizational strength.

The staffs vary from state to state in size, professional background and training, and amount of turnover. Over 2000 persons are employed by SPAs. Approximately 68 percent are professional employees and 29 percent are clerical employees. The permanent professional staff size ranges from six in Hawaii to sixty-six in California, with a national average of twenty-six. In the study of professional employees listed in the 1977 planning documents, we determined the educational background and previous occupation of key staff members such as the director, assistant director(s), research, evaluation, and planning directors, and the chief planner for police, courts, juveniles, and corrections. Internal administrative employees, such as auditors, were excluded.

It might be expected that persons with degrees in criminal-justice specialties would represent the values of organizations in the criminal-justice functions whereas persons with degrees in other fields wuld have the broader systemic orientation that LEAA espouses. For each state, table 3-3 lists the percentage of key professional employees in 1976 who have degrees in a criminal-justice specialty versus general degrees. In all but three states, there are more people with general than with specialist degrees. There are also many persons with no degree or with degrees not falling into these classifications. In order to measure functions' organizational strength, a second indicator is necessary.

Table 3-3

Occupational Background and Degree Background of SPA Staff, 1976
(N=43)

State	% with Criminal-Justice Specialist Degrees	% with Generalist Degrees	% with Criminal-Justice Experience	% with Generalist Experience
Alabama	3.2	9.7	3.2	22.6
Alaska	0	66.7	33.3	44.4
Arkansas	0	18.2	13.6	13.6
California	0	12.0	12.0	4.0
Colorado	14.3	35.7	21.4	21.4
Connecticut	4.0	16.0	–	–
Delaware	0	5.9	17.6	11.8
Florida	0	4.9	2.4	4.9
Georgia	0	20.8	8.3	16.7
Hawaii	–	–	50.0	0
Idaho	7.1	50.0	35.7	14.3
Illinois	1.8	5.3	7.0	1.8
Indiana	–	–	23.1	11.5
Iowa	5.6	33.3	16.7	27.8
Kansas	6.7	13.3	13.3	13.3
Kentucky	0	18.8	18.8	9.4
Maine	0	14.8	3.7	14.8
Maryland	13.3	16.7	26.7	6.7
Massachusetts	9.6	1.9	17.3	1.9
Minnesota	3.6	17.9	7.1	10.7
Mississippi	11.1	5.6	–	–
Missouri	8.7	4.3	13.0	8.7
Nevada	0	10.0	30.0	0
New Hampshire	9.1	18.2	0	63.6
New Jersey	0	8.2	8.2	2.0
New Mexico	18.2	54.5	54.5	36.4
New York	5.7	5.7	11.3	3.8
North Carolina	3.3	10.0	3.3	3.3
North Dakota	0	38.5	30.8	7.7
Ohio	3.6	18.2	9.1	10.9
Oregon	0	16.7	0	25.0
Pennsylvania	0	3.5	1.2	2.3
Rhode Island	0	26.1	4.3	17.4
South Carolina	13.0	17.4	17.4	21.7
South Dakota	0	41.7	25.0	25.0
Tennessee	3.8	26.9	19.2	15.4
Texas	5.2	5.2	5.2	5.2
Utah	6.7	6.7	6.7	13.3
Vermont	6.3	18.8	12.5	31.3
Virginia	–	–	5.5	5.5
West Virginia	0	19.4	6.5	6.5
Wisconsin	0	7.4	0	7.4
Wyoming	0	10.0	20.0	10.0

Note: Specialist degrees = Law, CJ; Generalist degrees = Social science, business, education, humanities, sciences; Criminal-Justice Experience = Police, courts, corrections, juvenile; Generalist experience = Government, politics, education, military, business; – = missing.

It is also appropriate to examine whether employees had prior experience in the criminal-justice field, which might make them amenable to their old friends' interests, or whether they worked in other jobs which might generate a broader perspective. This information is also included in table 3-3. In eighteen states, the largest proportion of employees had criminal-justice experience; in fifteen states, general experience was more typical. It should also be noted that the SPA is many employees' first job. Also, many employees could not be classified in this manner.

Overall, the professional employees are such a mixture that it would be very difficult to use their characteristics as indicators of functional organizational strength and penetration into the staff. Their turnover is fairly rapid as well, so while table 3-3 is descriptively interesting, it is not a good indicator of organizational access to SPA's decision making.

RPUs and CJCCs. Besides the SPAs at the state level, regional planning units exist for substate regions and, since 1971, criminal-justice coordinating councils exist for larger cities and counties. States are required to pass through 40 percent of their Part B planning monies to these planning units unless LEAA deems it inappropriate. Some CJCCs receive Part C (action) monies in addition. RPUs are established by SPAs and they also have small staffs and advisory boards. Generally the boards exert more influence than the staff on the regional level because regional staffs are often composed of one or two part-time workers. States vary a good deal in the amount of discretion allowed the regional units, ranging from states that approve each application at the state level to those that make mini-block grants to regions. The mini-block-grant feature, a victory for the cities, is incorporated in the Carter administration's recent bill. It appears from the ACIR study that about half of the states are presently centralized in terms of planning and, in the other half, planning is decentralized to the regional level.[32] Nevertheless, about two-thirds of those responding to the ACIR survey said that the SPA, not the RPU or CJCC, has the most influence in determining which activities and jurisdictions receive funding.[33]

There are approximately 1000 people employed by RPUs, 56 percent of whom are professionals. The total professional staffs range in size from 1 to 133, averaging 22 across the nation. The sum of all RPU employees in a state is slightly less than the average-sized SPA staff, though somewhat more RPU employees perform clerical functions than do SPA employees. RPUs are not included in the later empirical analysis because they are not as important as the SPA staff in the state allocation process, and the available data on them are not complete.

Federal Strategies of Influence with State
Criminal-Justice Systems

While the SPA, the disbursor of federal funds, is the target of recipient organizations, it is also the federal government's change agent in the state criminal-justice system. As a change agent, it is the target of federal attempts to ensure that the allocations it makes are consistent with federal directives. The strategies that the federal government uses when trying to change state criminal-justice systems—either directly or indirectly through the SPA—are described here.

The Exchange Strategy. The exchange strategy involves the infusion of complementary goals and values into the organization one is trying to change. That is, one organization tries to control or influence another by ensuring that the two organizations' members share norms and values. A frequent way of fostering such similarity, particularly in a dispersed organization system, is professionalization. LEAA has encouraged the training of practitioners and creation of a new profession of planners. Now we want to see, on a state-by-state basis, how well the federal government is doing in achieving professionalism.

At the time the data were collected (1976), only a handful of SPA employees had degrees in criminal-justice planning. Typically, employees had either a general degree or experience in criminal justice. We reasoned that the level of education is the more important dimension of professionalism from the standpoint of LEAA. They want the SPAs to "shake up" the state systems not just employ people who come directly out of the system. SPAs whose employees are highly educated are more likely to share the systemic outlook of LEAA than are SPAs whose employees are less well educated. These education scores will be used later on as one indicator of SPA professionalism.

The ranking of SPAs according to education of key professional employees is given in table 3-4. An MA would seem to be the minimal qualification for undertaking the systems analysis and comprehensive planning that LEAA demands. There are only eleven states whose average level is that of an MA or above (a score of at least 2.00). Most states have SPAs whose key employees, on average, have a college degree; two states have SPAs whose top personnel, on average, did not finish college. It is hard to imagine that these two SPAs could plan and make allocations in the manner LEAA envisioned.

Presumably LEAA would also like to imbue RPUs with professional norms and values. Available data indicate that this task is proceeding much more slowly. Table 3-5 shows the states arrayed according to their average educational scores for RPU employees in 1976. Since these units are so small (one or two people), this average generally refers to the director's education. In no state is the average that of an MA; in most states the average employee has a BA; in six states the average is less than a college degree. Although RPUs do not figure in the later analysis, it could be predicted that if structural changes give more power to RPUs, federal directives are less likely to be followed than they are now.

Table 3-4
Ranking of SPAs According to Education Score, 1976 (*N*=44)

State	Education Score
Hawaii	2.67
Illinois	2.50
New York	2.50
Minnesota	2.43
South Carolina	2.10
Kentucky	2.08
Texas	2.00
Wisconsin	2.00
New Jersey	2.00
Maryland	2.00
Florida	2.00
Colorado	1.89
Ohio	1.88
Mississippi	1.83
Missouri	1.83
Massachusetts	1.78
Oregon	1.75
Connecticut	1.71
New Mexico	1.60
North Carolina	1.57
Vermont	1.57
Virginia	1.57
Arizona	1.50
Georgia	1.50
Idaho	1.50
Iowa	1.42
Delaware	1.40
California	1.40
West Virginia	1.38
Alaska	1.33
Kansas	1.33
Utah	1.33
Pennsylvania	1.33
South Dakota	1.29
Arkansas	1.25
Wyoming	1.25
Rhode Island	1.25
Tennessee	1.20
Maryland	1.14
New Hampshire	1.13
Indiana	1.00
North Dakota	1.00
Nevada	.80
Alabama	.64

Source: Calculated by authors from 1977 Planning Documents of states.

Note: Education score is calculated as follows: PhD or JD = 3; MA = 2; BA = 1; less than BA = 0.

Table 3-5
Ranking of States According to Educational Scores of Regional Planning Units, 1976 (N=26)

State	Score
Colorado	1.92
Pennsylvania	1.50
Connecticut	1.47
Kentucky	1.46
Maryland	1.45
Utah	1.43
Tennessee	1.38
Georgia	1.38
Oregon	1.33
New Mexico	1.33
California	1.33
Minnesota	1.32
South Carolina	1.32
Michigan	1.29
Missouri	1.26
Kansas	1.25
Louisiana	1.15
Virginia	1.13
South Dakota	1.00
Wyoming	1.00
Iowa	.86
Illinois	.79
Nebraska	.75
Maine	.71
Alabama	.50
Arkansas	.22

Source: Calculated by authors from 1977 Planning Documents of states.

The exchange strategy is also directed at the three criminal-justice functions—police, courts, and corrections. The best measure of the professionalism of each function on a state-by-state basis would be the average level of training for employees, comparable to the data on SPA professionals. These data unfortunately do not exist for all functions for all states. Instead, the average salary was used as an indicator of professionalism of each function.[34]

The Power-Dependency Strategy. In addition to the exchange strategy, the federal government has a second strategy for exerting power over target organizations: making them dependent on the federal government. Primarily this occurs through manipulation of their resources' flow. At the state level, LEAA has two weapons: the block-grant funds (planning and action) and the discretionary funds. The block-grant funds are a much larger dollar amount but their allocation is fixed by formula. The discretionary funds are smaller in total amount but their allocation to states is by definition discretionary. Both large amounts and variable amounts have the potential for creating dependencies.

Block-grant Funds. The largest amount of money the federal government disburses is in block-grant funds, Part B for SPA planning, Part C for action funds, Part E for corrections, and Part J for juveniles. The planning funds constitute nearly all the budget of SPAs and hence the change-agent organization is very dependent on LEAA. No SPA director believes his agency would survive without LEAA funding.[35] It was assumed that all SPAs are equally dependent on LEAA and their responsiveness to federal directives varies only with their level of professionalism.

The block-grant action funds are the major "carrot" that LEAA has for the state and local criminal-justice organizations. Their effectiveness, however, is limited in two ways: SPAs control the allocation of action funds to projects, so the attainment of federal objectives is dependent on SPA professionalism; and action funds constitute a small proportion of a state or local organization's total budget, so dependence is low. In early years when the program was small, LEAA funds were around 2 to 3 percent of state and local criminal-justice expenditures. In later years, action funds were over 5 percent of nationalwide expenditures.[36] For this reason, compliance with federal directives can be expected to increase over the time period studied. Compliance, however, may decline in the future if LEAA's appropriations continue to decline.

These national averages conceal much variability in dependence by function and state. The later analysis focuses on each state's criminal-justice system's dependence on LEAA funds: dependence contributes to the attainment of federal directives. The measure of dependence is the proportion of a state system's annual budget that comes from the SPA. It was assumed that organizational systems in a scarce resource environment respond to the availability of even small amounts of money. Therefore, highly dependent(on SPA funds) functions will carry out SPA directives. Functions with little dependence on SPA funds are free to ignore SPA directives. In such a case the exchange strategy is the only possible compliance mechanism.

Discretionary Funds. The second inducement at LEAA's disposal is the award of discretionary funds. From LEAA's perspective the advantage of discretionary funds is that their allocation is determined by LEAA centrally, not by SPAs. Federal preferences can be directly implemented. Their disadvantage as a compliance mechanism is that they are a small amount of money. Discretionary funds constitute 15 percent of Part C action funds and 50 percent of Part E action funds. They are disbursed by LEAA to state and local units of government with the approval of the SPA in that state. Official documents state that:

Discretionary funds are veiwed as the means by which the Law Enforcement Assistance Administration can advance national priorities, draw
attention to problems not emphasized in State plans, and provide
special impetus for reform and experimentation within the total law
enforcement improvement structure created by the Act. Discretionary
funds represent only a small portion of the total aid that will be available to State and local government and, thus, will be used for special
emphasis and supplementation rather than to meet the massive or
widespread need that State plans and "block grant" action funds must
address.[37]

A later chapter discusses the impact of discretionary funds, centering on
the flow of discretionary monies into states as a strategy by which the national
government attempts to control its target network of criminal-justice organizations. The indicator of this form of dependence is the amount of discretionary
funds per capita awarded to a state.

Our hypothesis is that states that receive more than their population's share
of discretionary funds tend to follow federal directives more closely than do
states that receive proportionately smaller amounts of funds. It is assumed that
discretionary funds, like block-grant action funds and planning funds, create
dependence on the part of recipient organizations; dependence leads to compliance with federal directives. Dependence is a function of the size of the resource, discretion in its allocation, and the number of alternative sources for
money. For criminal-justice organizations, alternative sources of resources are
the state and local governments. They are also likely to be the source of directives that conflict with federal guidelines. Criminal-justice organizations, therefore, are subject to conflicting local, state, and federal directives. They will be
responsive to those directing organizations on which they are most dependent.

State Government Strategies of Influence over
Criminal-Justice Systems

State governments direct their attempts at influencing the criminal-justice system
toward three targets: state and local functional organizations, and the SPA itself.
Compared to cities, state governments are new to this game, beginning with the
arrival of the block grant in 1968. They are trying to maintain control over their
own state agencies (state police, correctional institutions, and state court systems), set statewide standards for local agencies (city and county police, local
jails, and lower courts), and make the SPA into a state agency (that is, responsive
to state directives) rather than a federal agency.

State Agencies. The state's first targets are the state agencies, which are the
easiest to control. State officials are used to this battle. State agencies are over-
whelmingly dependent on the state, which provides 95 percent of their budgets.

Local Agencies. The second targets, local agencies, are harder to control. Traditionally, local governments have provided most of the criminal-justice services, spending 61 percent of the total criminal-justice budget. The combination of local fiscal pressure (now intensified by property-tax revolt) and inability of local governments to perform satisfactorily has led to demands for reform. Many of these suggested reforms involve the state, either in the operation, regulation, or financing of local criminal-justice services. In the last ten years, state involvement in previously local services has increased, most dramatically in the courts area.[38]

SPAs. The third target of state influence, the SPA, is probably the hardest to control. Such control efforts are directly relevant to the concerns of this book: they reflect state governments' attempts to regain influence lost when the federal government introduced its change agent, the SPA, into the states' organizational matrix.

The available generic strategies are the same for the state government as for the federal: exchange and power dependence. The chief state actors are the governor, the state legislature, and the other state criminal-justice agencies. In pursuing an exchange strategy, all three state actors would prefer that the SPA be staffed with persons whose views are complementary to theirs. The governor uses the exchange strategy most successfully as he or she appoints the SPA director who in turn appoints the staff. Though all but the top positions are civil-service positions, it was discovered that the SPA director tends to mold the staff in his or her own image. That is, if the director is a retired military man, his staff tends to have more than the usual number of former military officers. (Beyond this example, we do not have the kind of information which would allow a comparison of state officials' views with SPA staffs' views.)

In pursuing a dependence strategy, state actors do not have much power over the SPAs since 90 percent of planning and action funds come from the federal government. A number of states, however, provide planning funds in excess of the required amounts. In those states, it might be expected that there is independence from federal control and acquiescence to state control: Alaska, Kentucky, and Pennsylvania all provide more than 40 percent of the SPA's budget; Illinois, Massachusetts, Nevada, and New Mexico all provide more than 30 percent of the SPA's funds.[39]

In the LEAA program state actors tend to concentrate on controlling the resource of authority rather than money. Most actions by governors and legislatures try to change the basis and substance of the SPAs' authority rather than its funding source. Originally SPAs were created by executive order and were often thought of as governors' agencies, that is, as staff. In 1976 Congress required that SPAs be created by statute (that is, legislatively created). Also Congress gave state legislatures review powers, though not veto power, over SPA programs. These congressional actions provide a powerful resource to the state in its struggle to control the SPA. It can reorganize the agency, change its name, relocate it within state government, or give it additional functions to perform. In this manner the Kentucky SPA has probably been the most integrated into its state-government structure.

One measure of state attempts to exert control over the SPA might be the number of major SPA reorganizations (indicating a dependence strategy) and the number of new SPA directors (indicating an exchange strategy). We have calculated the number of changes from 1970 to 1977 in leadership (though the count does not capture the situation where the directorship changed more than once in a year) and numbers of major reorganizations as indicated by changes in agency names. As table 3-6 shows, reorganization and turnover have been substantial—in one case, eight times in seven years. Such organizational flux creates an impression that the SPA is a temporary group to be shuffled around rather than a permanently-operating organization. Such a status rebounds to the detriment of the SPA. In the interviews a state criminal-justice-agency head's view of an SPA director was given: ". . . a real professional won't work for a temporary agency like the SPA so they get some kid right out of college who tells us that he will shape us up. We say 'get lost buddy.' Why should I listen to someone who is temporary?"[40]

The interviews with organizations representing states confirmed this description of SPA-state relations. They are uninterested and uninfluential in SPA decision making. Governors are not involved in the day-to-day operation of the SPAs, and many are not interested in increased involvement because so little money is at stake that it is not worth their time. Furthermore, legislators are more negative about LEAA than they are about any other federal program.[41] State lawmakers want some input into the initial SPA funding decisions since state and local governments are expected to fund the successful projects after the third year. In 1977, for example, 80 percent of the projects considered eligible for continuation support were continued by recipient units of government.[42] As the ACIR study reported, moreover, the perceptions of SPA directors are congruent with a description of state actors as powerless: the governor and especially the state legislators were rated as having the lowest influence among participants in SPA policymaking.[43]

Overall, state actors try without much success (though their success is increasing over time) to control the authority of SPAs. Both their resources for exerting influence and interest in influencing the SPA are limited. They are somewhat better at regulating local criminal-justice activities and controlling state criminal-justice agencies. They are more interested in these organizations' operations and have greater resources to affect them. To go further than noting these general practices would require a survey of all state and local criminal-justice participants. Other governments are also trying to control these systems of organizations. The federal impact is not achieved in a vacuum. The effect of a given amount of federal pressure on the criminal-justice system may vary from state to state, depending on each state government's amount of pressure on the same system.

Table 3-6
Ranking of SPAs According to Number of Reorganizations and
Changes in Directors, 1970 to 1977

State	Number of Changes
Alaska	8
North Carolina	7
New York	7
Pennsylvania	6
Kentucky	6
Michigan	5
Florida	5
Oregon	5
Ohio	5
Vermont	5
Colorado	5
California	4
Texas	4
South Dakota	4
Rhode Island	4
Oklahoma	4
North Dakota	4
Mississippi	4
Connecticut	4
Georgia	3
Delaware	3
Massachusetts	3
Missouri	3
New Mexico	3
Nebraska	3
South Carolina	3
Wyoming	3
Wisconsin	3
West Virginia	3
Washington	2
Tennessee	2
Utah	2
New Jersey	2
Iowa	2
Indiana	2
Illinois	2
Arkansas	2
Alabama	2
Arizona	1
Idaho	1
Louisiana	1
Kansas	1
Maryland	1
Maine	1
New Hampshire	1
Nevada	1
Montana	1
Minnesota	1
Virginia	1
Hawaii	0

Source: Calculated by authors from LEAA Annual Reports.

Issues in the Block-Grant Program

Three sets of issues emerge from the examination of congressional hearings, interviews with interest group participants, and other scholars' assessments of LEAA's performance: functional allocation, jurisdictional allocation, and the substantive goals of the program. The functional groups are directly involved in arguing over the share that each function gets from the SPA subgranting process. Likewise, the jurisdictional groups argue about the share that each level of government receives from the subgranting process at the state level. Other actors tend to focus on whether the program has succeeded in reducing crime, stimulating innovation, and building a criminal-justice system out of diverse elements.

Functional Allocation. During every congressional reauthorization period, controversy develops over the share of action funds allocated to each adult criminal-justice function: police, courts, or corrections. Each functional sector has argued for a larger share of the pie, and the criticism most often heard is that the police get too much. Table 3–7 shows the proportion of action funds nationwide going to each of the three functions. Indeed, police did get a large share in the first year of the program (79 percent). Two factors explain the large share initially given to police by SPAs. In the first year, the police were probably the only component sufficiently organized to submit large numbers of grant proposals to SPAs; and according to congressional mandate, LEAA was initially a law-enforcement program with special emphasis on riot control and organized crime.

Table 3-7
Distribution of LEAA Block-Grant Awards by Criminal-Justice Component, Fiscal Years 1969 to 1977, Percent of Funds Awarded

Year	Police	Courts	Corrections	Total
1969	79	8	13	100[a]
1970	64	8	27	100
1971	50	12	38	100
1972	47	17	37	100
1973	46	16	37	100
1974	44	19	37	100
1975	45	19	36	100
1976	40	23	37	100
1977	41	26	33	100

Source: General Accounting Office as quoted in U.S., Congress, Congressional Budget Office, *Federal Law Enforcement Assistance: Alternative Approaches* (Washington, D.C.: Government Printing Office, 1978), p. 9.

[a]Detail may not add to total because of rounding.

Congressional sentiment seems to have been that 79 percent was too much for police because, in late 1970, Congress earmarked a separate category, E, for corrections and required that states maintain the previous level of correctional effort in Part C as well. Similarly, the 1976 Congress said that an "adequate" share of action funds must be given to the courts function. Table 3-7 demonstrates that these categorization amendments and SPA actions resulted in a decline in the police share to 41 percent by 1977, an increase for courts from 8 percent to 26 percent, and an increase for corrections from 13 percent to 33 percent. Certainly the 1977 figures show a more balanced allocation of funds. Whether each sector now believes its share to be fair, however, is another matter.

Jurisdictional Allocation. The question of jurisdictional allocation is a second controversy that has emerged in every congressional reauthorization and manifested itself in every state. Federal money is allocated to the SPA. It then reallocates (subgrants) it to state, city, county, and in some instances private agencies. Controversy focuses on the aggregate share of action funds obtained by the state, city, and county levels in the subgranting process. Whereas the most frequent criticism in the functional allocation process is that the police get too much, here the most frequent criticism is that the state gets too much.

During the 1967 hearings on the Safe Streets Act, the block-grant concept was opposed because the states historically have had fewer law-enforcement responsibilities than the cities and counties. The argument for the block grant, however, included the reasoning that states could provide the coordination necessary to bring together the fragments of the criminal-justice system. The cities and counties have been fighting this new state role ever since, and their best chance of success was in the 1979 reauthorization under a Democratic president. The cities began their counterattack in the very first set of hearings in 1970 with a report concluding that the program is a failure because it neglects the cities where 85 percent of the crime takes place.[44] In 1973, the cities' report argued that local governments are not partners with the state but are forced into the roles of supplicant and beggar.[45]

Similarly, the counties allege that they spend more on criminal justice (35 percent) than does any other level of government (state, federal, or local) and that they unfairly receive a very small percentage of LEAA monies.[46] It is true that, except for the police function, counties outspend cities for functions such as corrections, legal services, indigent defense, and judicial services. However, according to LEAA publications, county total expenditures are less than municipal spending.[47]

The ACIR evaluated the joint complaint of cities and urban counties that they are not receiving their fair share of action funds from SPAs. It concluded that money is generally allocated according to the crime rate.[48] For example, cities over 100,000 received 57 percent of action funds, have 57 percent of the crime but only 45 percent of the population. If their findings are correct, it blunts the force of the urban governments' argument that they deserve more money. Urban governments make a similar complaint that they don't get a fair share of the planning funds. They argue that they should be able to determine their own priorities and submit a single plan for funding instead of submitting separate projects. This mini-block-grant concept was enacted by the 1979 amendments.

Success of the Program. The third area of controversy is not generated by an internal conflict among criminal-justice interests but results from the external attack that argues that LEAA is "a waste." LEAA has been charged with wasting money on fancy police gadgets, being badly organized, and wallowing in red tape.[49] Basically, such criticisms argue that LEAA is not reaching its goals. These attacks threaten the survival of the program and the orderly flow of resources to this organizational system. We ask, What accounts for the agency's degree of success or failure in reaching its goals? On the basis of our theory, characteristics of LEAA's organizational system can be identified that would either facilitate or hinder its program. The earlier propositions predict the conditions under which states would achieve the agency's goals.

The first step is to discover the goals of the criminal-justice block grant, that is, the yardsticks by which accomplishment is measured. The goals may be found in congressional testimony at the time of the agency's establishment, the agencies' annual reports, and in general discussions by scholars of the goals of block grants. On these bases, three major goals of the LEAA program have been identified: the reduction of crime, innovation, and building a criminal-justice system.

Reduction of Crime. As stated in the original act and repeated in congressional testimony, LEAA's primary goal is the prevention and reduction of crime. Since the crime rate continued to go up until recently, it is generally agreed that the agency has not accomplished this goal. The agency admits defeat, as the 1979 bill purposefully excludes prevention or reduction of crime as a goal.

Two defenses are offered for the agency. First, LEAA monies have led to great improvements in state and local crime-reporting systems. A substantial, though indeterminate, share of the rise in crime rate is due to better reporting of crimes committed. Second, the determinants of the crime rate lie outside the scope of the criminal-justice system and cannot be remedied by money, especially the small amounts involved in the LEAA program. For example, two important determinants of the crime rate are the size of the youth population and the rate of unemployment within that group. The Congressional Budget Office found that the numbers of youth and unemployment explained 97 percent of the variation in the U.S. Crime Index.[50]

Innovation. A second identifiable, though less prominent, goal is innovation, especially through research and demonstration projects. Although LEAA might not have enough money to fight crime directly, it is argued, its money could be imaginatively used to demonstrate new techniques in crime fighting. The discretionary funds especially could be used in this fashion. Then state and local governments could continue the best of these experiments from their own monies.

Overall, LEAA has been more successful in inducing innovation than in reducing crime but whether that is an accomplishment sufficient to justify its existence is still disputed. Congressional testimony indicates that any program new to a state would be considered innovative and, by that criterion, 59 percent of the projects are innovative.[51] Any better assessment of the degree of innovation would require a detailed analysis of every project description and evaluation of its results.

System Building. A third identifiable goal of LEAA is that of system building: making the various components of criminal justice into a coordinated and improved set of functions which constitutes a system. The 1968 act expressed this goal as coordination. It was implemented through requirements for comprehensive planning and representation of all criminal-justice components on SPA boards and through reliance on the SPA to unify the various components. Over the years, Congress has repeated its emphasis on system building. On opening the 1973 hearings, Chairman Peter Rodino said: "We who framed the Omnibus Act recognized that it was hopeless to expend time and energy aimed at improving this or that aspect of law enforcement. Rather we felt that the criminal justice system as a functioning interrelationship of police, courts and correctional facilities needed coordinated planning and reform."[52] The block grant's encouragement of system building is also one of its presumed advantages over revenue sharing and categorical aid. Statewide planning for the block grant provides opportunities for coordination and communication between criminal-justice functions, as well as between jurisdictions.[53]

Evaluation of progress in system building is somewhat easier than evaluation of success in crime reduction or innovation. Participants generally agree that the system is now more integrated and interdependent, though the causes for these changes are not agreed on.[54]

The organizational actors defend the program against charges that it has not reduced crime, been innovative, or built a system. At the same time, they argue among themselves over the fairness of allocations to functions and governments.

Alternative Views of the Policy Process

The case for an interorganizational perspective on the criminal-justice system has been documented. Having established the congruence of the theory and the real world, the consequences of the theory can be investigated. It has been shown that it is realistic to assume that organizational interactions do matter.

Yet one might object that the policy process can be viewed differently. Further, one might argue that we must empirically reject all alternative theoretical explanations in order to establish the validity of the theoretical and empirical analysis.

Obviously, we are in no position to undertake this mammoth task in one book. What we can do, however, is to engage in the exercise of imagining what the policy process would look like if organizations were not important. If the hypothetical conditions describe the real world, then the theory is not going to fit the real world.

Hypothetical Structural-Policy Process at National Level

The other actors who might significantly affect the outcome of the structural-policy process include the president, Congress, the agency, department, and political parties. These actors are often significant in other policy areas.

The origin of the idea for the LEAA program was a Democratic president (Johnson) and the program was further supported by the Republican presidents Nixon and Ford. Carter, a Democrat, is the first president to oppose the program. While a candidate, he accused LEAA of wasting millions of dollars "while making almost no contribution to reducing crime."[55] Once in office, however, Carter was unable to kill the program. Nixon had also unsuccessfully tried to convert the program into a revenue-sharing program. Though a president was instrumental in initiating the program, subsequent presidents have had less influence on it. Thus an analyst would not discover much about the current structure of the program by studying the presidency.

The second set of actors that usually looms large in setting up structure consists of members of Congress. A few individuals have played significant roles due to their committee assignments. Policymaking in the Senate centers around the Judiciary Committee, chaired by John McClellan until his death in 1977, and currently chaired by Edward Kennedy. McClellan and Roman Hruska were instrumental in writing the original legislation and McClellan often took the Senate floor to defend the agency against its critics. Kennedy authored the last reauthorization bill and has tried unsuccessfully to raise LEAA's current budget. Policymaking in the House centers around Emanuel Celler's Judiciary Committee, currently chaired by Peter Rodino.

Aside from these few individuals, however, congressional interest in LEAA is low. It is so low, in fact, that House Democrats began the 1979 session with three vacancies on the Judiciary Committee. Judiciary was one of the three least popular committees among House applicants (including Ethics and District of Columbia), partly because the issues that the Judiciary Committee takes up are not politically attractive.[56] If interest in this committee stays at this level for long, it will help to ensure organizational dominance in the structural-policy process.

A third actor who is usually significant in altering the structure once it is in place is the department or agency. LEAA is part of the Justice Department which is headed by the attorney general. Though they have differeed in philosophy and political party, all but one of the attorneys general have supported the program. The most recent attorney general, Griffin Bell, is said to oppose the program even more than Carter does.[57] Bell, however, discovered that he could not abolish this agency within his own department.

Though LEAA is part of the Justice Department, daily operations are conducted by the LEAA administrator, not the attorney general. It is doubtful that agency heads have contributed materially to LEAA's survival. The lack of clear leadership is the most common criticism voiced in the interviews and scholarly assessments. Originally the agency was administered by a bipartisan "troika." This arrangement was modified in the 1970 amendments and eliminated in the 1973 amendments. The troika arrangement prevented much action at all, whereas the frequent changes in leadership thereafter brought frequent changes in policy directions, such as the shift in national emphasis from Pilot Cities to Impact Cities to initiatives. Since Carter came into office in January 1977, the agency has been run by an acting administrator, a guarantee of agency impotence.

The final set of actors that can be identified as potentially significant consists of the political parties. Has crime been an issue over which the two parties have clashed? The answer is, of course, no. The Safe Streets Act and its extensions have passed by very large margins. None of the votes reflect partisan divisions. The only partisan differences are in matters of policy implementation. The Democrats have tended to support amendments that would direct the flow of funds to the urban areas, whereas the Republicans originated the block-grant concept and supported the state role consistently. The compromises enacted in legislation have resulted in bipartisan support.

Thus none of these actors has had sustained impact on the structure of the process. In fact, the program was reauthorized in December 1979 even though the president and attorney general opposed it, there was no agency head to defend it, members of Congress in general did not want to deal with it, and no political party supported it. Still it is possible that these actors are powerful at the state level where the resources are allocated.

Hypothetical Allocation-Policy Process at the State Level

On the basis of our knowledge of other state-policy processes, there are several candidates for influential determinants of state policy: the socioeconomic environment, the governor, the legislature, political parties, and the agency (SPA). Most of these actors have already been discussed in previous descriptions of the process and the observations are summarized here.

While the socioeconomic environment often functions as a resource constraint in other policy areas, the state's wealth cannot, by definition, determine the level of resources in a federally-funded program. Certain parts of the state's environment might, however, constitute a demand for criminal-justice policy, that is, a high crime rate signifies a need for crime-fighting programs and may lead to a demand for such programs. As already indicated, crime rate is incorporated into the analysis as an indicator of need.

Since the SPAs' programs are primarily funded by the federal government, governors and legislatures have had little interest in or control over the SPAs. Recently they have attempted to exert more control as they realized its long-term impact on the state's budget, but so far they have not succeeded in determining the allocational patterns.

Most policy studies have found political parties to be of little consequence in determining state expenditures in various areas. Similarly, there is no indication that parties are active in allocating this money.

One might also speculate that the SPA is the primary determinant of resource allocation. After all, it does the allocating. In later chapters allocation patterns' relationships to SPAs' characteristics are investigated. At this point we can only note that no other scholars have concluded that the SPAs successfully dominate their task environments. Feely et al. characterize the SPA as the classic "man in the middle." If they are too closely allied with criminal-justice agencies, they are unnecessary; if they try to be strong leaders, they are too isolated and ineffectual.[58]

Notes

1. *Congressional Quarterly Almanac* (Washington, D.C.: Congressional Quarterly, 1972), 27:787.

2. U.S., Congress, House, Committee on Judiciary, *Law Enforcement Assistance Administration*, 94th Cong., 2nd sess., 1976, pp. 298-299.

3. The Advisory Commission on Intergovernmental Relations examined the cities' discretionary funding patterns and found no relationship with the mayors' political party: U.S., Advisory Commission on Intergovernmental Relations, *Safe Streets Reconsidered: The Block Grant Experience 1968-1975* (Washington, D.C.: Government Printing Office, 1977), p. 140.

4. Robert H. Salisbury and John Heinz, "A Theory of Policy Analysis and Some Preliminary Applications," in *Policy Analysis in Political Science*, ed. Ira Sharkansky (Chicago: Markham Publishing Co., 1970), pp. 39-60.

5. U.S., Department of Justice, Law Enforcement Assistance Administration, *Expenditure and Employment Data for the Criminal Justice System, 1976* (Washington, D.C.: Government Printing Office, 1978), p. ix.

6. Ibid., p. 7.

7. International City Management Association, *The Municipal Yearbook, 1974* (Washington, D.C.: International City Management Association, 1974), p. 226.

8. Ibid., p. 225.

9. U.S., President's Commission on Law Enforcement and Administration of Justice, *The Challenge of Crime in a Free Society* (Washington, D.C.: Government Printing Office, 1967), p. 14.

10. U.S., Advisory Commission on Intergovernmental Relations, p. 10.

11. *Congressional Quarterly Almanac* (Washington, D.C.: Congressional Quarterly, 1969), 24:235.

12. U.S., Congress, House, Committee on Judiciary, *Anti-Crime Program*, 90th Cong., 1st sess., 1967, pp. 1438-1449.

13. Ibid., pp. 1422-1423.

14. U.S., *Statutes at Large*, vol. 82, pp. 197-198.

15. Interview, 12 June 1978.

16. U.S., Advisory Commission on Intergovernmental Relations, p. 17.

17. Ibid., p. 23.

18. Interview, 14 June 1978.

19. See: National Conference of State Criminal Justice Planning Administrators, "Halting the Invasion of Categorization in the Crime Control Act Program . . . Why the Block Grant?," (Washington, D.C.: National Conference of State Criminal Justice Planning Administrators, 1977).

20. Interview, 28 June 1978.

21. Ibid.

22. Interview, 7 June 1978.

23. Interview, 14 June 1978.

24. James Q. Wilson, *Thinking About Crime* (New York: Vintage Books, 1975), p. xix.

25. *Congressional Quarterly Weekly Reports,* 15 July 1978, p. 1822.

26. Ibid., p. 1821.

27. *Congressional Quarterly Weekly Reports,* 26 May 1979, p. 1011.

28. These provisions are described in *Congressional Quarterly Weekly Reports,* 22 December 1979, pp. 2899-2900.

29. Interview, 12 June 1978.

30. U.S., Advisory Commission on Intergovernmental Relations, p. 57. Some states checked multiple responses.

31. Ibid., p. 58.

32. Ibid., p. 81.

33. Ibid., p. 84.

34. Wilson found that the police of Nassau County were the second highest paid in the state of New York and exhibited a service orientation different from other communities he studied: James Q. Wilson, *Varieties of Police Behavior* (Cambridge, Mass.: Harvard University Press, 1968).

35. U.S., Advisory Commission on Intergovernmental Relations, p. 95.

36. U.S., Congress, Congressional Budget Office, *Federal Law Enforcement Assistance: Alternative Approaches* (Washington, D.C.: Government Printing Office, 1978), p. 35.

37. U.S., Congress, House, Committee on Judiciary, *Law Enforcement Assistance Amendments*, 91st Cong., 2nd sess., 1970, p. 438.

38. Other changes are described in detail in Daniel Skoler, *Organizing the Non-System* (Lexington, Mass.: Lexington Books, D.C. Heath and Co., 1977).

39. U.S., Advisory Commission on Intergovernmental Relations, p. 99.

40. Interview, 14 June 1978.

41. Interview, 15 June 1978.

42. U.S., Law Enforcement Assistance Administration, *Ninth Annual Report, Fiscal Year 1977* (Washington, D.C.: Government Printing Office, 1978), p. 156.

43. U.S., Advisory Commission on Intergovernmental Relations, p. 127.

44. U.S., Congress, House, Committee on Judiciary, 1970, p. 18.

45. U.S., Congress, House, Committee on Judiciary, *Law Enforcement Assistance Administration*, 93rd Cong., 1st sess., 1973, p. 225.

46. National Association of Counties, *American County Platform and Resolutions* (Washington, D.C.: National Association of Counties, 1977), p. 123.

47. U.S., Department of Justice and Department of Commerce, *Trends in Expenditure and Employment Data for the Criminal Justice System 1971–1974* (Washington, D.C.: Government Printing Office, 1976), p. 5.

48. U.S., Advisory Commission on Intergovernmental Relations, pp. 140–142.

49. *Congressional Quarterly Weekly Reports*, 3 March 1979, p. 366.

50. U.S., Congress, Congressional Budget Office, p. 12.

51. U.S., Advisory Commission on Intergovernmental Relations, p. 133.

52. U.S., Congress, House, Committee on Judiciary, 1973, p. 2.

53. Carl W. Stenberg and David B. Walker, "The Block Grant: Lessons from Two Early Experiments," *Publius* 7(Spring 1977):55.

54. U.S., Advisory Commission on Intergovernmental Relations, p. 95.

55. *Congressional Quarterly Weekly Reports*, 3 March 1979, p. 366.

56. *Congressional Quarterly Weekly Reports*, 27 January 1979, p. 155.

57. Interview, 12 June 1978.

58. Malcolm Feeley, Austin Sarat, and Susan White, "Implementation of the Safe Streets Act: The Role of State Planning in the Development of Criminal Justice Federalism," mimeographed, no date, p. 30.

Research Design

The Role of Interorganizational Theory
in the Empirical Research

Interorganizational theory has achieved wide acceptance in sociology as an explanation of organizational behavior. The empirical work cited in chapter 2 demonstrates that the organizational characteristics of an organization's environment affect its behavior, in addition to the effects of internal organizational characteristics. In political science, empirical research has shown that internal organizational characteristics affect the behavior of political organizations, including its policy outputs.[1] It is a short and a logical step to assert that environmental factors will affect the behavior, including the policies, of political organizations. Indeed several sociologists and political scientists have suggested as much.[2] To our knowledge no one has actually conducted empirical research explaining public policy on the basis of interorganizational factors, despite the shared belief that the explanation may be appropriate.

Despite this belief, an interorganizational explanation would not be appropriate for all policy areas. For example, those that are highly economically or rationally determined would be excluded from its reach. In order to be included, a policy area must satisfy the basic assumptions of organizational importance and interaction. In chapter 3 a lengthy analysis established that the criminal-justice-policy process at both the national and state levels is dominated by large organizations that are mutually aware. Further, the federal government directs its strategies toward these large organizations. It is appropriate to treat federal policymakers as attempting to manipulate these large organizations' environments.

In the chapters 5, 6, and 7 the theory is applied, not tested. Propositions are deduced from the theory (such as those about power dependency and exchange as federal strategies), and these are used to predict policy outcomes. The statistical results allow us to make statements about the power of organizations and success of federal strategies. The results do not allow the rejection of interorganizational theory. To do that the propositions would have to be tested on a number of different policy areas and the range of the theory's applicability tested. Instead the propositions are applied to fifty different states in order to learn the conditions under which the strategies work best.

The approach in this book can be compared to that of empirical research using rational or economic theories. Research in voting behavior, for example, does not test the assumption of rationality on the part of citizens in their choice of vote (though sometimes the assumption is tested in experiments designed for that purpose). Rather hypotheses about the behavior of voters and leaders are deduced and compared with "real-world" behavior. The purpose here is similar. The difference is that we have shown the assumptions of our theory are realistic, while rational choice models generally fail on this score.[3]

Research Design

Interorganizational theory is used to predict behavior in three cases: functional allocations of SPA-action funds, innovative projects funded by SPAs, and joint projects between different functions. In each case the direction in which the federal government wishes the states to move is specified first: to allocate less to police and more to courts and corrections; to be more innovative, especially on national priority projects; to undertake more joint projects. The justifications for these goals as federal directives are explained in chapters 5, 6, and 7.

Modeling Strategy

The exchange and dependence strategies are modeled separately (propositions 1 and 3). Dependence is modeled as blocked by organizational strength (proposition 2). The interaction of exchange and dependence is modeled also (proposition 4). The general equations are

Proposition 1. Federal directive = f (dependence).

Proposition 2. Federal directive = f (dependence, organizational strength).

Proposition 3. Federal directive = f (exchange).

Proposition 4. Federal directive = f (exchange, dependence).

The allocation of relatively more to the federally-directed policy choice is conceived of first as a function of dependence on federal funds. Then the relation of federal directives to dependence is allowed to be altered by organizational strength. Third, the federal directive is conceived of as a function of exchange represented by professionalism. Lastly, the relationship between following federal directives and exchange is allowed to be mediated by dependence.

These general propositions can be represented by a series of regression equations.

$$Y = a + b_1 X_1 + b_2 X_2 + e \qquad (1)$$

where Y = federal directive,
X_1 = fixed dependence,
X_2 = discretionary dependence,
e = error term.

Equation 1 says that the tendency of a state's organizational system to follow federal directives is a linear and additive function of the dependence of that system on federal funds, including both those allocated by formula and by discretion.

$$Y = a + b_1 X_1 + b_2 (X_2 \cdot X_1) + e \qquad (2)$$

where Y = federal directive,
X_1 = the most important form of dependency from equation 1,
X_2 = a dummy variable representing organizational strength: $X_2 = 1$ if strength is above the median; $X_2 = 0$ if strength is below the median.
e = error term.

The effect of organization strength is to change the slope; that is, to alter responsiveness to federal directives. The following of federal directives is a function of dependence and its interaction with organizational strength. Equation 2 allows high organizational strength to increase the steepness of a positive slope. The dependence variable selected is whichever variable had the largest beta coefficient in equation 1. This is done to conserve degrees of freedom, which dwindle rapidly with only fifty cases and several independent variables.

The exchange strategy is modeled as follows:

$$Y = a + b_1 X_1 + b_2 X_2 + e \qquad (3)$$

where Y = federal directives,
X_1 = SPA professionalism,
X_2 = functional professionalism,
e = error term.

Equation 3 says that the tendency of a state's organizational system to follow federal directives is a linear and additive function of shared professional norms between the federal government and SPAs and between the federal government and each criminal-justice function.

$$Y = a + b_1 X_1 + b_2 (X_1 \cdot X_2) + e \qquad (4)$$

where Y = federal directives,
X_1 = the most important form of exchange from equation 3,
X_2 = a dummy variable for dependency: $X_2 = 1$ if the state is above the median on the best form of dependence selected in equation 1; $X_2 = 0$ if the state is below the median on the selected measure of dependence,
e = error term.

The following of federal directives is a function of the exchange relationship established by professionalism and its interaction with dependence. High dependence increases the positive slope of the exchange relationship. In order to conserve degrees of freedom, the best measure of dependence is selected from equation 1 and the best measure of exchange from equation 3.

Equations 1 and 3 test the dependence and exchange strategies, respectively, as separate strategies. If the signs of the coefficients are as predicted, a comparison of the R^2's indicates which strategy is the more effective. Equations 2 and 4 are straightforward tests for interaction. If the signs of the dummy-variable coefficients are in the predicted direction and statistically significant, they show that organizational strength can alter dependence and that dependence can alter exchange.

In the course of the empirical work a large number of more complicated formulations were considered. The equations presented here, however, parsimoniously but accurately represent the theoretical propositions outlined in chapter 2. Their simplicity is an important virtue, as the four equations will be tested for three different dependent variables over several time periods.

The modeling of interaction emerged after considerable experimentation and discussion. Several alternative procedures for testing interaction were tried but rejected in favor of dummy variables. Their advantages are multiple: they provide a straightforward interpretation of the coefficients, a better specification of the model, and conserve degrees of freedom.[4] Although it is possible to add a dummy variable to a multiple-regression equation consisting of several independent variables, the one best-fitting variable for interaction was selected. Otherwise there would be an interactive term for each independent variable and soon the number of variables would begin to equal the number of cases. For each dependent variable there is the possibility that the effect of the interactive term is to shift the intercept or both the intercept and slope. The results of these two equations are reported only where they provide a better fit than does the version suggested by our theory: the dummy variable alters only the slope.

The alternatives to dummy variables are separate regressions within each category of the dummy variable or a multiplicative nonlinear model. For two reasons separate regressions were not run. Degrees of freedom are lost and the test for the effect of the control variable is not obvious. A multiplicative model was rejected because the resultant substantive interpretation is so strained. For the dummy variables, however, the two regression lines can be shown graphically, one for each value of the dummy variable.

In the empirical chapters the models of exchange and dependence are analyzed, along with measures of incrementalism and rationality. The federal strategies are working in a policy process constrained by many other factors. Two general explanations (incrementalism and rationality) have been provided by other investigators. Where there is an annual data series for the dependent variable, the impact of incrementalism is estimated as well as of the exchange and dependence strategies of federal influence. In order to examine the degree of rationality in policymaking, a measure of policy need is added to the inter-organizational equations. To conserve degrees of freedom, incrementalism and rationality are included in further equations only if their predictive capacity was high in the first equation. Incrementalism and rationality are conceived of being linear and additive in their relation to the following of federal directives.

Selection of Time Periods

Policy is a process and any empirical specification should reflect the dynamics of the process.[5] Consequently one of the oldest block-grant programs was selected for the analysis. Still, the ten-year period is too short for time-series regression. The few available degrees of freedom would constrain severely the comparison of alternative multiple-regression models. Yet the block-grant program has changed greatly over the years and many relationships among the variables of interest may have changed over time. Thus several cross-sections are used to look at changes in relationships across time. For one set of dependent variables (functional allocations), annual data from 1969 to 1976 is analyzed. For joint projects the 1973 and 1976 data are analyzed separately. Other years were impossible to obtain. For innovations, which involve small amounts of money, data over all available years were averaged.

Measurement of Concepts: Independent Variables

We began this study by criticizing the unreflective empiricism of the early state-policy studies. Ideally, it would be preferable to extend the multiple-indicators approach to measurement from its familiar use in survey research to aggregate data, where it is seldom used.[6] As the study began, we hoped to be very explicit about the degree to which the indicators measured the concepts: conceptual clarity and precision of measurement were dual goals.

We discovered in the process of data collection and preliminary analysis, however, that available data do not meet the high standards of this approach. It was difficult to develop the same number of indicators for each concept. There were often missing data on an item. In a survey the researcher can eliminate those cases with missing items—but, in research like this, one cannot very well throw out several states on each of a number of indicators. Sometimes, we had to average across several indicators, each of which had some missing information, in order to get one measure of a concept. Attaining the precision of the multiple-indicator model is, therefore, impossible. About all that can be done is to assess the face validity of each indicator by looking at the ranking of the states on each dimension. Where possible, validity is assessed also by correlating the selected indicator with another indicator in the data set.

The reliability of the measures is primarily a function of the data-gathering capacity of LEAA. The coding was done by the senior author from published reports of LEAA, its in-house documents, and computer-based data system. The appendix lists each data source and discusses any known biases or difficulties. Our experience in getting access to LEAA data was interesting. Officials were initially helpful but as they became acquainted with the research purposes, they expressed reservations. Their reaction was, "You can't tell anything from these data." On hearing out their specific objections (detailed in the appendix), we still believe that the data are sufficiently reliable for our purposes. The data represent an underlying dimension.

Perhaps LEAA officials were concerned that their data would make them "look bad." Indeed, as chapter 8 suggests, LEAA does look bad on some dimensions of performance. Yet their objections to the conclusions surely would be much greater if we were using data gathered by another source. After all, we are using the agency's data gathered for their own purposes. If there is any bias in the data collection, it should be in the direction of making the agency look good, not bad.

Measurement of the Exchange Concept. Chapter 3 describes how the exchange strategy works through professionalism and demonstrates that the most important professional organizations are the SPA and the agencies within each criminal-justice function. The measurement of professionalism in the SPA and in each function in each state is described here.

SPA Professionalism. The rankings of the states on the average education of the members of their SPAs was reported in chapter 3. The score reflects an important dimension of professionalism. From the same 1977 planning document, data were obtained on two additional items representing other dimensions of professionalism: the salaries of the same key individuals included in the education ranking and the amount of money that the SPA devotes to library materials and subscriptions. These three indicators capture the different elements of professionalism: that is, persons who are highly educated, earn high salaries, and read journals (or at least have access to them) have the norms and values of a professional community. In addition to their face validity as an indicator of this construct, these three indicators had the highest intercorrelations among the potential indicators of professionalism that were available: education-salary, $r = +.34$; education-subscriptions, $r = +.44$; salary-subscriptions, $r = +.43$.

The data for these indicators were collected from each state's planning application for 1977, a document written in 1976. The documents are housed in LEAA's library in Washington, D.C. Where an item was missing, the SPA was contacted to obtain the missing information. Complete information was obtained for forty-two states and data for at least one indicator are present for all states.

These three indicators, which have different metrics, were combined into one measure by taking the mean of their standard scores. The professionalism index, shown in table 4-1, places New York, Wisconsin, and Illinois at the top while Oklahoma, Nebraska, and Louisiana fall at the bottom of the ranking. The ranking of the states is congruent with our impressions of SPAs' reputations.

We preferred to have an indicator of the SPA's professionalism in early years of the block-grant program. The 1976 plan, however, was the only year in which LEAA required relevant information to be reported. In the analysis, it must be assumed, therefore, that relative differences in professionalism have remained constant over the years, that is, that a professionalism ranking of the states in 1970 would be roughly the same as the one reported for 1976. In 1976, an SPA's professionalism score is correlated ($r = +.51$) with the size of its professional staff in 1976. That professional staff in 1976, in turn, is highly correlated ($r = +.72$) with size of the staff in 1970. The stability of this over-time relationship indicates that an SPA's degree of professionalism is fairly stable over time. Moreover, even if an SPA's 1976 score is an unreliable measure of its 1970 professionalism, the most likely consequence is that the estimated relationships in the early years will be less strong than the actual relationships.

Functional Professionalism. The only indicator available for the professionalism of each of the three functions is the average salary for all employees in that function. Fortunately, salary is usually considered to be an important indicator of professionalism.[7] The average salary is used to construct two different types of measures of professionalism. In explaining functional allocations, a ratio that compares each function to the other two is used. In explaining innovation and coordination, an average for the entire criminal-justice system is used.

The *ratio measure* is the proportion of total criminal-justice payroll allocated to a function, divided by the proportion of total criminal-justice employees employed in that function. Thus if the police in a state receive 50 percent of the total criminal-justice payroll but have only 40 percent of the criminal-justice employees, then their ratio of relative professionalism is 1.20. This ratio measure has the advantage of showing one function's professionalism relative to other functions in that state. If the average salary for each function in a state had been used instead, it would have reflected only the status of each profession nationwide (that is, judicial salaries would be higher than police salaries which would be higher than corrections salaries). In order to explain why one criminal-justice function receives more money from the SPA than another, a measure is needed that shows the degree to which judicial salaries exceed other salaries in one state. Then there is a basis for comparison with the judicial sector's salary advantage in other states.

The ratio-salary measure does correlate with other dimensions of professionalism in each function. Police salary correlates modestly with the average number of hours of training police officers received in 1976 ($r = +.28$); court salary

Table 4-1
Ranking of States on SPA Professionalism, 1976

Rank	State
1	New York
2	Wisconsin
3	Illinois
4	Texas
5	Hawaii
6	New Jersey
7	Florida
8	Pennsylvania
9	Alaska
10	Virginia
11	California
12	Minnesota
13	Arizona
14	Colorado
15	Maryland
16	Oregon
17	South Carolina
18	Georgia
19	Ohio
20	Massachusetts
21	Missouri
22	Delaware
23	Kentucky
24	Iowa
25	Michigan
26	Connecticut
27	Idaho
28	New Mexico
29	Rhode Island
30	Utah
31	Mississippi
32	North Carolina
33	West Virginia
34	New Hampshire
35	Nevada
36	Indiana
37	Wyoming
38	Vermont
39	Kansas
40	Arkansas
41	Washington
42	Alabama
43	Tennessee
44	Maine
45	South Dakota
46	North Dakota
47	Montana
48	Oklahoma
49	Nebraska
50	Louisiana

Source: Calculated from data in state-planning applications for 1977.

correlates strongly with the size of the court administrator's professional staff ($r = +.60$); and corrections salary correlates negatively (as it should) with the turnover rate among correctional employees ($r = -.35$). These correlations indicate that the salary-based measure captures the dimension of professionalism that LEAA is trying to encourage: criminal-justice functions with high relative salaries are likely to be more professionalized, and therefore to be more responsive to LEAA.

In the analysis of innovation and coordination, a measure of overall professionalism among the criminal-justice employees in the state, rather than a ratio measure comparing functions is needed. For this purpose, the mean annual salary for all criminal-justice employees in the state is used. These figures should be reliable. They are averages of large numbers of employees. Table 4-2 reports the rankings of the states in 1973 and 1976 on this overall measure of functional professionalism. In the top five spots in 1976, Alaska and Hawaii have high prices, and California, Michigan, and New York are all large states with well-paid employees. The bottom five states are either Southern or border states. Even though variations in cost of living may contribute to the rank orderings of states, still the rankings are congruent with the impressions of peer evaluations of states' criminal-justice employees.

Measurement of Concept of Dependence. An organization is responsive to another organization to the degree the former is dependent upon the latter for resources, money, and authority. LEAA has relatively large but fixed block-grant funds to offer state criminal-justice organizational systems. It has relatively small but variable non-block-grant funds to offer as well. These funds are kept distinct because we want to be able to determine whether the block-grant format or the categorical format (represented by the discretionary funds) is more effective in stimulating organizational systems to respond.

Fixed Dependence. Measures of dependence have been employed by the ACIR in its studies and by Hale and Palley.[8] Both have found it to be useful in explaining responsiveness to state and federal control. It should be important also in explaining acquiescence to federal directions. LEAA's budget has increased over most of the time of the research for this book. Consequently, the importance of its funding to state and local agencies should have increased over time, as should their dependence on it. Fixed dependence is measured by the proportion of a function's state and local budget that comes from its SPA. Data for this measure are available on an annual basis from LEAA reports. Since the fiscal reporting at this level of aggregation is good, these data are reliable. Table 4-3 reports the ranking of the states on fixed dependence for 1969 to 1972 and 1973 to 1976 for criminal justice overall.

In the period 1973 to 1976 those states that are most dependent on federal funds in the criminal-justice area are the poorer states: Arkansas, West Virginia,

Table 4-2
Ranking of States on Criminal-Justice Average Salary, 1973, 1976

Rank	1973	1976
1	Alaska	Alaska
2	New York	California
3	California	New York
4	Michigan	Michigan
5	Illinois	Hawaii
6	Nevada	Maryland
7	Connecticut	Nevada
8	New Jersey	Minnesota
9	Maryland	Illinois
10	Minnesota	Massachusetts
11	Massachusetts	Washington
12	Hawaii	Arizona
13	Pennsylvania	Oregon
14	Wisconsin	Wisconsin
15	Oregon	New Jersey
16	Washington	Pennsylvania
17	Delaware	Colorado
18	Rhode Island	Connecticut
19	Arizona	Rhode Island
20	Ohio	Delaware
21	Colorado	Iowa
22	Vermont	Florida
23	Florida	Utah
24	New Hampshire	Ohio
25	Virginia	Texas
26	Missouri	Virginia
27	Utah	Nebraska
28	Iowa	Kentucky
29	Nebraska	New Hampshire
30	Texas	New Mexico
31	Indiana	Vermont
32	Kentucky	North Dakota
33	Georgia	Montana
34	North Carolina	North Carolina
35	Maine	Missouri
36	New Mexico	Wyoming
37	North Dakota	Indiana
38	Alabama	Idaho
39	Tennessee	Louisiana
40	South Dakota	Tennessee
41	Idaho	Georgia
42	Louisiana	Alabama
43	Kansas	Maine
44	Montana	South Dakota
45	Wyoming	Oklahoma
46	South Carolina	Kansas
47	West Virginia	South Carolina
48	Mississippi	West Virginia
49	Oklahoma	Mississippi
50	Arkansas	Arkansas

Source: Calculated from data in U.S., Department of Justice, Law Enforcement Assistance Administration, *Expenditure and Employment Data for the Criminal Justice System* (Washington, D.C.: Government Printing Office, 1970-1978).

Table 4-3

Ranking of States on Block-Grant Funds as a Percent of Total State and Local Criminal-Justice Expenditures, 1969-1972, 1973-1976

Rank	1969-1972	1973-1976
1	West Virginia	Arkansas
2	Arkansas	West Virginia
3	North Dakota	North Dakota
4	Mississippi	Wyoming
5	Wyoming	South Dakota
6	South Dakota	Mississippi
7	Idaho	Alabama
8	Alabama	Indiana
9	Kentucky	Oklahoma
10	Iowa	New Hampshire
11	South Carolina	Kentucky
12	New Hampshire	Maine
13	Utah	Idaho
14	Oklahoma	Tennessee
15	Montana	Iowa
16	Tennessee	Texas
17	Maine	Utah
18	Indiana	South Carolina
19	Nebraska	Nebraska
20	Georgia	North Carolina
21	North Carolina	Georgia
22	Texas	Minnesota
23	Virginia	Montana
24	Kansas	Virginia
25	Vermont	Ohio
26	Ohio	Missouri
27	Louisiana	Pennsylvania
28	Missouri	Wisconsin
29	Rhode Island	Kansas
30	New Mexico	New Mexico
31	Colorado	South Carolina
32	Pennsylvania	Vermont
33	Washington	Washington
34	Wisconsin	Connecticut
35	Connecticut	Louisiana
36	Oregon	Delaware
37	Florida	Oregon
38	Delaware	Illinois
39	Michigan	Michigan
40	Arizona	Colorado
41	Massachusetts	Florida
42	Illinois	Hawaii
43	Minnesota	New Jersey
44	New Jersey	Maryland
45	Maryland	Arizona
46	Hawaii	Massachusetts
47	Alaska	New York
48	California	California
49	Nevada	Alaska
50	New York	Nevada

Source: Calculated from block-grant data in U.S., Department of Justice, Law Enforcement Assistance Administration, *Annual Report of the Law Enforcement Assistance Administra-*

Table 4-3   continued

tion (Washington, D.C.: Government Printing Office, 1969-1975); 1976 block-grant data from PROFILE system; state and local expenditure data in U.S., Department of Justice, Law Enforcement Assistance Administration and U.S., Department of Commerce, Bureau of the Census, *Expenditure and Employment Data for the Criminal Justice System* (Washington, D.C.: Government Printing Office, 1970-1978).

North and South Dakota, and Wyoming. Less dependent are the larger and more populous states of Massachusetts, New York, and California, as well as Alaska and Nevada. Although these states may receive more federal dollars in absolute terms, federal funds constitute tiny percentages of their large state budgets for criminal justice. The states' relative positions have not changed much over time.

Variable Dependence. Each state's value on the measure of fixed dependence is determined by the block-grant formula, though the SPA allocates these monies within the state. A small portion of Part C and half of Part E funds are retained by LEAA and disbursed centrally. These discretionary funds are the only resource that LEAA directly allocates, and so might be used in different ways than block-grant funds. Discretionary funds are intended to advance national priorities, while block-grant funds are intended to advance state and local priorities.

Table 4-4 reports the ranking of states on per capita–discretionary funds received over two periods, 1969 to 1972 and 1973 to 1976. Most of the small states are toward the top of the ranking and thus are dependent on LEAA's discretion. Their position is due to LEAA's practice of giving a discretionary supplement to states that are too small to afford an SPA on the basis of their planning funds alone. There are no external checks on the validity of this dimension of dependence, though the fact that LEAA controls its allocation provides face validity for it as an indicator of variable dependence. If this form of dependence is more important in bringing about responsiveness to federal demands than dependence on the larger block grants, then we may conclude that the categorizing of the program would bring compliance with federal norms.

Measurement of the Organizational-Strength Concept. *Organizational strength* refers to the ability of an organization to marshal its resources of size and political clout to block other organizations and acquire more resources for itself. Each function in a state is conceived of as pitted against other functions as they struggle to acquire resources from the state government. A proportional measure, therefore, should express the strength of each function relative to the other two. One of the measures, derived from the state budget, indicates the relative success of each function in lobbying the governor and state legislature. Another measure, based on number of personnel in each function, indicates the number of potential voters to which a legislature and governor respond. These data are taken from annual agency publications and should be reliable at this highly aggregated

Table 4-4
Ranking of States on Discretionary Grants Per Capita, 1969-1972, 1973-1976

Rank	1969-1972	1973-1976
1	Alaska	Alaska
2	Delaware[a]	Colorado
3	Nevada[a]	Hawaii[a]
4	Colorado	Nevada[a]
5	Idaho	Wyoming[a]
6	Wyoming[a]	Arizona
7	Arizona	Oregon
8	Montana[a]	Maryland
9	New Mexico	Delaware[a]
10	Maryland	Montana[a]
11	New Hampshire[a]	South Dakota[a]
12	Louisiana	Vermont
13	Rhode Island	New Mexico
14	North Dakota[a]	Nebraska
15	Vermont	Georgia
16	Oregon	New Jersey
17	Florida	Oklahoma
18	South Carolina	Missouri
19	Missouri	Idaho
20	Hawaii[a]	New Hampshire[a]
21	Alabama	Utah
22	West Virginia	Kentucky
23	Georgia	Michigan
24	Maine	Louisiana
25	South Dakota[a]	North Dakota
26	California	Maine
27	Nebraska	Illinois
28	Mississippi	Florida
29	Ohio	New York
30	Kentucky	California
31	New Jersey	Massachusetts
32	Utah	Ohio
33	Massachusetts	Arkansas
34	Arkansas	Alabama
35	Texas	Texas
36	Minnesota	Rhode Island
37	Michigan	Minnesota
38	Oklahoma	Virginia
39	Connecticut	Pennsylvania
40	Kansas	South Carolina
41	New York	Washington
42	Virginia	Wisconsin
43	Pennsylvania	Iowa
44	Washington	Kansas
45	North Carolina	Indiana[a]
46	Illinois	North Carolina
47	Wisconsin	Connecticut
48	Indiana[a]	Tennessee[a]
49	Tennessee[a]	West Virginia
50	Iowa	Mississippi

Source: Calculated from data in U.S., Law Enforcement Assistance Administration, *Sixth Annual Report of the Law Enforcement Assistance Administration, Fiscal Year 1974* (Washington, D.C.: Government Printing Office, 1974), pp. 214-215; *Eighth Annual Report of the Law Enforcement Assistance Administration, Fiscal Year 1976* (Washington, D.C.: Government Printing Office, 1977), pp. 91, 96.

[a]Receives small state supplement.

level. The final measure averages these two components: the proportion of state and local expenditures for the criminal-justice system allocated to each function, and the proportion of state and local criminal-justice full-time employees in each function. This variable is dichotomized at the median so it can be used as a dummy variable. The dummy variable's advantage is that it provides a straightforward test for interaction. For each function this measure represents the relative organizational clout of police, courts, and corrections in each state. The two components of this measure are more highly interrelated with each other than with other possible indicators of each function's strength (the intercorrelations range from +.75 to +.86).

According to table 4-5, the states ranked in the top five on the police organizational-strength index in both time periods are Illinois, Mississippi, and New Hampshire. In these states, the police consistently capture a relatively large share of the state and local budget and employ a large number of people. The police function in these states is probably more politically powerful than corrections and judicial functions. At the bottom of the scale in both periods are Delaware and Alaska. Their police are likely to be weaker politically than judges or corrections officials.

Table 4-6 gives the same information for the corrections function. Less stability in the rankings is evident than was found in the police rankings, perhaps because of fairly dramatic improvements—often, court ordered—in some of the more notorious prison systems. North Carolina is the only state in the top five in both periods, indicating that its corrections function has more clout, relative to other criminal-justice functions, than in other states. Illinois and Hawaii, on the other hand, consistently rank at the bottom in corrections organizational strength.

The organizational strength of judges is arrayed by state in table 4-7. Alaska, North Dakota, and West Virginia are consistently toward the top of the scale and South Carolina and Maryland toward the bottom. Judges probably have more political strength compared to criminal-justice personnel in the top states and less strength in the bottom states.

There is a problem in assessing the validity of these measures of relative strength within the states since most existing indices compare absolute strength across states. For the court area, however, there is one possibility for checking validity: the method of *judicial selection*. Bar associations have long advocated the removal of judicial selection from the partisan political arena. The institutionalization of this reform (either nonpartisan election or the merit plan) demonstrates judicial clout and prestige. Hence, states with much party inflence and little bar influence in judicial selection (that is, appointment, partisan election, or legislative election) should rank low on the measure of organizational strength. States with much bar influence and little party influence in selection should rank high.[9] Such a tendency does exist: of the states with *reformed selection* (that is, merit or nonpartisan), fifteen rank above the median and eleven fall below the median. Of the states with *unreformed selection* (that is, partisan), ten fall above the median and fourteen fall below. For this reason, we are satisfied with the index's validity.

Table 4-5
Ranking of States on Police Organizational Strength, 1969 to 1972,
1973 to 1976

Rank	1969-1972	1973-1976
1	Mississippi	West Virginia
2	Arkansas	Illinois
3	Illinois	Mississippi
4	Rhode Island	Hawaii
5	New Hampshire	New Hampshire
6	New Jersey	Rhode Island
7	New York	Connecticut
8	Kentucky	Massachusetts
9	Louisiana	Alabama
10	Arizona	Missouri
11	Hawaii	New Mexico
12	Connecticut	New York
13	Nebraska	Maine
14	New Mexico	Kentucky
15	Texas	Arkansas
16	Indiana	Utah
17	Alabama	Wisconsin
18	Michigan	Indiana
19	Pennsylvania	New Jersey
20	Massachusetts	Louisiana
21	Utah	Michigan
22	Virginia	Arizona
23	Maryland	Texas
24	South Carolina	Oklahoma
25	Wisconsin	Iowa
26	Oklahoma	Pennsylvania
27	West Virginia	Minnesota
28	Nevada	North Dakota
29	Idaho	Wyoming
30	Iowa	Nebraska
31	Florida	Tennessee
32	Missouri	Idaho
33	North Dakota	Maryland
34	South Dakota	Virginia
35	Tennessee	South Dakota
36	Wyoming	Colorado
37	Ohio	South Carolina
38	Maine	Ohio
39	Minnesota	Nevada
40	Kansas	Washington
41	Montana	Montana
42	California	Georgia
43	Georgia	North Carolina
44	Washington	Florida
45	Oregon	California
46	North Carolina	Vermont
47	Colorado	Oregon
48	Delaware	Kansas
49	Vermont	Delaware
50	Alaska	Alaska

Source: Calculated from data in U.S., Department of Justice, Law Enforcement Assistance Administration, and U.S., Department of Commerce, Bureau of the Census, *Expenditure and Employment Data for the Criminal Justice System* (Washington, D.C.: Government Printing Office, 1970-1978).

Table 4-6
Ranking of States on Corrections Organizational Strength, 1969 to 1972,
1973 to 1976

Rank	1969-1972	1973-1976
1	Vermont	North Carolina
2	North Carolina	South Carolina
3	Washington	West Virginia
4	Alaska	Virginia
5	California	Georgia
6	Maryland	Vermont
7	Georgia	Kansas
8	Maine	Maryland
9	Minnesota	Washington
10	Kansas	Tennessee
11	Oregon	California
12	Delaware	Alaska
13	South Carolina	Florida
14	Tennessee	Nevada
15	Wisconsin	Montana
16	Virginia	Delaware
17	Montana	Oregon
18	Ohio	Ohio
19	Nevada	Maine
20	Wyoming	Wisconsin
21	Iowa	Minnesota
22	West Virginia	Iowa
23	Colorado	Arkansas
24	Massachusetts	Oklahoma
25	Utah	Wyoming
26	Kentucky	Utah
27	Florida	Connecticut
28	New York	Massachusetts
29	New Mexico	Idaho
30	Indiana	Indiana
31	New Hampshire	Nebraska
32	South Dakota	Kentucky
33	Michigan	Louisiana
34	Idaho	New Hampshire
35	Connecticut	Colorado
36	Pennsylvania	New York
37	Oklahoma	Pennsylvania
38	Louisiana	Michigan
39	New Jersey	Rhode Island
40	Texas	Mississippi
41	Nebraska	Arizona
42	Alabama	Missouri
43	Rhode Island	Alabama
44	Arizona	North Dakota
45	Missouri	South Dakota
46	Illinois	New Mexico
47	North Dakota	New Jersey
48	Arkansas	Texas
49	Mississippi	Illinois
50	Hawaii	Hawaii

Source: Calculated from data in U.S., Department of Justice, Law Enforcement Assistance
Administration, and U.S., Department of Commerce, Bureau of the Census, *Expenditure
and Employment Data for the Criminal Justice System* (Washington, D.C.: Government
Printing Office, 1970-1978).

Table 4-7
Ranking of States on Judicial Organizational Strength, 1969 to 1972,
1973 to 1976

Rank	1969-1972	1973-1976
1	Alaska	Alaska
2	North Dakota	North Dakota
3	Colorado	West Virginia
4	Hawaii	South Dakota
5	Delaware	Delaware
6	Idaho	Hawaii
7	South Dakota	Colorado
8	Oklahoma	Nebraska
9	Florida	Oregon
10	Montana	Idaho
11	Arizona	Pennsylvania
12	Oregon	Wyoming
13	Ohio	Montana
14	Pennsylvania	Kansas
15	Alabama	Michigan
16	Texas	Vermont
17	Nebraska	Rhode Island
18	Michigan	Iowa
19	Connecticut	Ohio
20	Georgia	New Jersey
21	Wyoming	Alabama
22	Iowa	Minnesota
23	Kansas	Texas
24	Louisiana	Florida
25	Vermont	Louisiana
26	Rhode Island	New Mexico
27	New Jersey	Arizona
28	West Virginia	California
29	Minnesota	Tennessee
30	Tennessee	Oklahoma
31	California	Washington
32	Nevada	Nevada
33	Indiana	Utah
34	New Mexico	Kentucky
35	Utah	Missouri
36	Illinois	Indiana
37	Washington	Connecticut
38	Massachusetts	Arkansas
39	Arkansas	Georgia
40	New Hampshire	New York
41	Wisconsin	Massachusetts
42	New York	Virginia
43	Missouri	New Hampshire
44	Maine	Illinois
45	North Carolina	Mississippi
46	Kentucky	Maine
47	Virginia	North Carolina
48	Mississippi	Wisconsin
49	South Carolina	Maryland
50	Maryland	South Carolina

Source: Calculated from data in U.S., Department of Justice, Law Enforcement Assistance
Administration, and U.S., Department of Commerce, Bureau of the Census, *Expenditure
and Employment Data for the Criminal Justice System* (Washington, D.C.: Government
Printing Office, 1970-1978).

Measurement of Control Variables. In chapter 2, the existence of two other explanations for allocations (incrementalism and rationalism) were discussed, and consequently the need to incorporate measures of their central explanatory concepts in the models. Incrementalism has been measured in the budgetary literature as the degree to which one year's allocation is based on the previous year's allocation (also called the *base*).[10] Where annual data are available, the previous year's SPA allocation is taken as the base for the following year's budget. If a high degree of incrementalism exists, it is difficult for SPAs to respond to federal directives.

The operational definition of rationality in the policy process has been more troublesome for scholars than that of incrementalism. Without entering into a longstanding debate over motives for human behavior, it is reasonable to assume that a rational policymaker would allocate resources on the basis of the severity of the problem. In the area of criminal-justice policy, therefore, resources would be allocated on the basis of the crime rate. LEAA has encouraged SPAs to engage in rational planning processes. Hence, allocations by crime rate would be in accord with federal guidelines as well as an expression of differing state needs. The magnitude of the crime rate indicates the intensity of the need for a solution.

Many agree that national resources should be rationally allocated according to need. For example, city spokespersons argue that since urban areas have most of the crime they should get most of the money. A different allocational problem exists at the state level. On the basis of the state's crime rate, how does a rational SPA planner decide which function should receive block-grant funds? How do we evaluate the degree of rationality that is evidenced in SPA allocational decisions? We are not prepared to argue that the police need more money if crime is high and that courts need more money if crime is low. Rather, our argument about need is more general. If the planning process is rational instead of incremental or political, the pattern of allocation will be similar in high-crime states and different from that in low-crime states. The magnitude of the crime problem will structure the allocation in some systematic but unspecified way.

Need for a solution is measured by the annual violent-crime index of the FBI (Federal Bureau of Investigation) which measures the crimes per 100,000 population. While crime statistics are often criticized for underestimating the true crime rate, these criticisms do not affect the use of the FBI's measure. The FBI index is a valid indicator of the construct need because it, not the true measure, is the measure SPA planners use in making decisions about allocations. Table 4–8 reports the violent crime rate for all states and arrays states consistently over time.

An additional advantage to this measure is that it allows a prediction about how the alternative formula adopted in 1979 might work in the future. That plan awards extra funds to seventeen high-crime states if the authorized funding level exceeds the present level. If the SPAs in high-crime states follow federal directives more closely, then a change to the new formula might result in increased compliance.

Table 4-8
Ranking of States on Violent-Crime Rate, 1969-1972, 1973-1976

Rank	1969-1972	1973-1976
1	New York	New York
2	Maryland	Maryland
3	Michigan	Nevada
4	Florida	Florida
5	California	Michigan
6	Illinois	California
7	Louisiana	Illinois
8	Missouri	Arizona
9	Nevada	New Mexico
10	Arizona	South Carolina
11	North Carolina	Alaska
12	Colorado	Louisiana
13	Texas	Missouri
14	New Mexico	North Carolina
15	Delaware	Georgia
16	Georgia	Colorado
17	New Jersey	New Jersey
18	Alaska	Massachusetts
19	South Carolina	Oregon
20	Alabama	Tennessee
21	Virginia	Texas
22	Tennessee	Delaware
23	Ohio	Alabama
24	Oregon	Ohio
25	Massachusetts	Washington
26	Washington	Mississippi
27	Arkansas	Virginia
28	Pennsylvania	Arkansas
29	Mississippi	Pennsylvania
30	Indiana	Indiana
31	Oklahoma	Rhode Island
32	Kentucky	Oklahoma
33	Rhode Island	Kansas
34	Kansas	Kentucky
35	Connecticut	Connecticut
36	Nebraska	Nebraska
37	Minnesota	Utah
38	Utah	Hawaii
39	Hawaii	Wyoming
40	Wyoming	Minnesota
41	Idaho	Idaho
42	Montana	Montana
43	West Virginia	Maine
44	South Dakota	South Dakota
45	Wisconsin	West Virginia
46	Maine	Wisconsin
47	Iowa	Iowa
48	Vermont	New Hampshire
49	New Hampshire	Vermont
50	North Dakota	North Dakota

Source: Calculated from data in U.S., Department of Justice, Federal Bureau of Investigation, *Uniform Crime Reports for the United States* (Washington, D.C.: Government Printing Office, 1968-1977).

The Nature of Cross-Sectional Data

While much of social-science research relies on goodness-of-fit tests for models, the nature of the problem in this book and the type of data used suggest that the goodness of fit will be naturally low, for statistical and theoretical reasons.

Regression analyses of cross-sectional data at an aggregated level usually yield low R^2's because aggregation reduces the variation from one unit to the next. There is not much that can be done about the reduced variation since the unit we are interested in is the organizational system, not the individuals in it. The R^2 is a measure of improvement in guessing over the mean so that the R^2 can be expected to be small whenever the mean is a good predictor.[11] In this case the mean for each dependent variable would be a relatively good predictor because the allocating agencies (the SPAs) are relatively homogeneous units set up at the same time by the federal government to do the same job in different states. The cross-sectional (static) nature of the data cannot be altered since too few observations exist to conduct regression analysis over time.

The R^2's for the exchange and dependence equations will be modest because of the nature of the theoretical approach. We deliberately focus on only one determinant of the policy outcome, the organizational system, so many potentially important factors are omitted. Hence, we cannot expect to explain as much of the extant variation as would a more complete model. The models will only fit well if the focal organization is an effective manager, that is, if its implementation of the strategies of exchange and dependence is successful in achieving the organization's goals. As already noted there are a number of indications that LEAA has not been a successful manager. If LEAA is not prestigious enough to establish an exchange relationship, then the dependent variable will not change in response to a small change in the professionalism measures. Additionally, the concept of the block grant has been criticized for its inability to change subnational policy outcomes. If the funds available in the block grant are not sufficient to create a dependency, then the allocations will not change in response to a small change in the dependence measures.

In view of these theoretical and statistical impediments to analyzing the relationships among variables, it is appropriate to focus on consistency and direction instead of the ability to explain variance. Do identifiable federal strategies of exchange and dependence alter the flow of resources? Does interaction among strategies or the mobilization of organizational strength alter the ongoing flow of resources? These sorts of questions direct attention toward changes in the partial regression coefficients under certain circumstances rather than toward the magnitude of the explained variance. Toward this end, the standard error of each slope coefficient is reported so that more weight can be placed on statistically significant coefficients and less weight on nonsignificant ones. Because there is no random sample of some larger universe, the use of significance levels may be questioned by some, despite their common usage in most state literature.[12]

We do believe that our findings should be regarded as more than a case study of LEAA-SPA relations in fifty sites. Campbell has argued that even a case study has scientific merit if the investigator's theory allows testing of several implications, that is, it is the number of tests, not the number of cases, that provides power to the results.[13] Since our method of investigation allows us to test multiple implications of our theory, we expand the degrees of freedom beyond the fifty states. Hence the findings are more than descriptive: they are generalizable. The .05 level of significance gives us a standard for deciding which relationships are generalizable.

Notes

1. James Q. Wilson, *Political Organizations* (New York: Basic Books, 1973); Donald S. Van Meter and Carl E. Van Horn, "The Policy Implementation Process," *Administration and Society* 6(February 1975):455–488.

2. Richard H. Hall, *Organizations: Structure and Process,* 2nd ed. (Englewood Cliffs, N.J.: Prentice-Hall, 1977); Jeffrey Pfeffer and Gerald R. Salancik, *The External Control of Organizations: A Resource Dependence Perspective* (New York: Harper & Row, 1978); Kenneth Hanf and Fritz W. Scharpf, eds., *Interorganizational Policy Making, Sage Modern Politics Series,* Vol. 1 (Beverly Hills, Calif.: Sage Publications, 1978).

3. For a critique on this score see: Terry M. Moe, "On the Scientific Status of Rational Models," *American Journal of Political Science* 23(February 1979):215–243.

4. Gerald C. Wright, Jr., "Linear Models for Evaluating Conditional Relationships, *American Journal of Political Science* 20(May 1976):349–373.

5. Virginia Gray, "Models of Comparative State Politics: A Comparison of Cross-Sectional and Time Series Analyses," *American Journal of Political Science* 20(May 1976):235–256.

6. Herbert L. Costner, "Theory, Deduction, and Rules of Correspondence," *American Journal of Sociology* 75(September 1969):245–273.

7. Michael Aiken and Jerald Hage, "Organizational Interdependence and Intraorganizational Structure," *American Sociological Review* 33(December 1968):912–931.

8. U.S., Advisory Commission on Intergovernmental Relations, *The Intergovernmental Grant System as Seen by Local, State, and Federal Officials* (Washington, D.C.: Government Printing Office, 1977); George E. Hale and Marian Lief Palley, "Federal Grants to the States: Who Governs?" *Administration and Society* 11(May 1979):3–26.

9. Kenneth N. Vines and Herbert Jacob, "State Courts and Public Policy," in *Politics in the American States,* eds. Herbert Jacob and Kenneth N. Vines, 3rd ed. (Boston: Little, Brown & Co., 1976): p. 251.

10. Otto A. Davis, M.A.H. Dempster, and Aaron Wildavsky, "A Theory of the Budgetary Process," *American Political Science Review* 60(September 1966):529–547.

11. Eric A. Hanushek and John E. Jackson, *Statistical Methods for Social Scientists* (New York: Academic Press, 1977), pp. 58–59.

12. Ramon E. Henkel, *Tests of Significance,* Sage University paper series on Quantitative Applications in the Social Sciences, series no. 07-001 (Beverly Hills: Sage Publications, 1976).

13. Donald T. Campbell, "'Degrees of Freedom' and the Case Study," *Comparative Political Studies* 8(July 1975):178–191.

5

The Allocation of Resources to Criminal-Justice Functions

This chapter examines the SPAs' allocation of block-grant funds to projects proposed by the three criminal-justice functions. This allocation process is central to a variety of perspectives. The outcome of the allocational process—particularly the share obtained by the police—has been the focus of much critical attention on the part of the public and Congress. Similarly, much of the political science literature has been devoted to analyzing the success of interest groups in obtaining resources for their constituents. The police's success in obtaining large shares of SPA funds is often attributed to the political strength of police organizations, especially their unions.

According to the theoretical literature on organizational behavior, the organization's desire to survive, which necessitates the acquisition of resources, motivates its behavior. Organizations seek resources in a number of ways, including interaction with other organizations. The theoretical perspective outlined in chapter 2 suggests a series of propositions that will guide our understanding of the politics of the allocational process. The federal government's power-dependency strategy is expected to have more effect on allocational patterns than will the exchange strategy.

The Concept of Functional Allocation

Throughout this book, we have accepted the Laswellian definition of politics as "who gets what, when, how." The allocation of a scarce resource among competing actors is therefore a political process. Political scientists have studied many different allocational dimensions: geographic, functional, per person, and so forth. While there are several potential allocational dimensions to the distribution of block-grant funds, only two have emerged as political disputes: functional (police, courts, corrections) and jurisdictional (city, county, state). One reason for the limitation is that only two types of competing actors are involved in this policy system: those representing the functional components of the criminal-justice system, and those representing the governmental (jurisdictional) levels. We justify our focus on the functional conflict on two grounds: our theory's focus upon functional interorganizational systems and the congruence between jurisdictions and functions (for example, local governments spend their money primarily on police).

The outcome of the functional-allocation process at the state level is well known: the police get the largest share; corrections, the second largest share; the courts, the smallest share. The police's share, however, has been declining over the years and allocation is becoming more balanced among the three functions. The reason for the success of the police, at the expense of the corrections and courts sectors, is not well understood. The results of the survey of the manpower level and the organizational activity in each sector suggests that the answer lies in the relative political strength of the police due to their larger numbers and unionization. This notion is investigated by analyzing the allocational patterns at the state level in relation to interorganizational differences among the three functions in the states.

Neither observers nor participants doubt that the allocational process is a political one whose outcomes are determined by the strength of the competing actors. Milward and Wamsley, contrasting the criminal-justice-policy network's formal tasks with its actual tasks, observe that its actual raw materials are the need for a plan and division of federal money without conflict. Its technology is log rolling, compromise, and symbolic politics to mask "business as usual."[1]

Participants in the policy process agree that the allocational process is a political one. The competing organizations representing the three functions, however, may have differential perceptions of the nature of the process. Possibly these perceptions depend on their success in obtaining the desired outcome for themselves. Publications from each functional area can be used to determine their assessment of the outcomes from SPA allocation of block-grant funds. Overall, no sector is satisfied with its share.

Police

A survey by the International Association of Chiefs of Police in the summer of 1977 summarized the attitudes of police chiefs toward the balance in LEAA funding. When asked whether LEAA funds are allocated fairly among the different functions, 19 percent agreed, 29 percent were not sure, and 53 percent disagreed.[2] However, when asked if LEAA funds should be used to support only law-enforcement programs, 54 percent disagreed, 8 percent were not sure, and 39 percent agreed. A majority of police chiefs do not expect to get all the money, but they do not think their share is large enough. The survey did not ask each chief what amount would be fair. One referent, however, might be the share that the police function gets from state and local governments. The nationwide average for police for the years 1972 to 1975 was 61.1 percent of the state and local dollars and 45.6 percent of the LEAA dollars. Perhaps something closer to 60 percent of the federal monies is what police chiefs have in mind.[3]

Courts

A 1975 report on LEAA support of the state courts labels their share as "separate but unequal."[4] Early on in the program, our interviews indicate, judges were not sufficiently organized to apply for grants: "Judges are just all thumbs when it comes to planning."[5] Also some sentiment existed among judges that they should not accept money from LEAA because of the separation-of-powers doctrine. If judges accept money from an agent of the executive (a commission appointed by the governor), some believe that their independence is compromised. Such sentiments, however, seem to be declining in strength.

It is hard to guess what percentage of funds would satisfy the judges. Already they have received more from LEAA in the period 1972 to 1975 (17.6 percent) than they did from state and local governments.[6] The representative of the Conference of Chief Justices testified that judges should receive a larger share of the SPAs' money but without competing with other functions to receive it. "The judiciary really ought to be looked after. Judges should not have to be politicians. If we allow politics to creep into the judiciary, then the rule of man will prevail instead of the rule of law."[7] Though his position did prevail (that is, court-planning funds were earmarked by Congress), it should be noted that other courts groups did not agree with this position. The Criminal Justice Section of the American Bar Association voted against separate judicial-planning funds, but they were overruled by a higher body in the ABA.

Corrections

In the corrections area, information on the function's evaluation of the fairness of its share is scanty. Corrections workers are the least organized of the three functions, and their association seems to have the least influence of those examined. The corrections function received more from LEAA (36.8 percent) in the 1972 to 1975 period than it did from state and local governments (25.1 percent).[8] One reason for their success in the competition for federal dollars was the national emphasis on community (residential) corrections facilities in the early 1970s. Deinstitutionalization was very popular in many states, where it was viewed as a cost-cutting move as well as a humanizing one. Another reason for their large share was the categorization amendment for corrections. This, however, was a suggestion of LEAA officials, rather than of corrections personnel.

As chapter 3 noted, Congress responded to the criticism of LEAA voiced by participants, observers, and its own members. In each congressional reauthorization (1970, 1973, 1976, and 1979), some categorization or earmarking of funds was accomplished. Seemingly, Congress was deliberately attempting to create some functional balance in the outcome of the allocation process. Thus Congress was no longer content to leave the allocation to the interplay of the SPA and the agencies seeking funds. By its actions Congress established a balanced allocation pattern as a federal directive. Given the nature of the initial imbalance, balance can only be achieved by giving less to police and more to the other functions. The figures presented in chapter 3 indicate that more functional balance has been achieved over the years. Such national figures, of course, could obscure many different degrees of functional balance within the states. In this chapter the interstate variation in functional balance is investigated. This is equivalent to investigating the degree to which states follow federal directives.

The Measurement of Functional Shares

Debates over the outcome of the SPA allocation process focus on the share of resources obtained by each function. Though much of political-science literature is concerned with the allocation of scarce resources, the typical measure of the outcome is the amount of expenditure, often on a per-capita basis or on a per-recipient basis. Such measures do not necessarily reflect the competition among actors since the individual recipient is not usually in a position to lobby on his or her own behalf. Similarly the aggregation of individual amounts to the system level (for example, the state) obscures the dynamics of competition because it ignores the intrastate, intergroup struggles that often determine allocation decisions. For these reasons, the outcome measure is the functional group's share of SPA action funds.

Organizations press their claims for more resources with two kinds of comparisons: interstate and intrastate. Some organizations argue for more money on the grounds that their state ranks low among states in expenditures toward a certain purpose. Similarly some organizations argue that their state justly ranks high and should be kept in that position. These interstate comparisons are justifications or means to an end—more resources for the group in question. Most comparative state-policy studies focus only on the interstate comparison. They fail to find much impact of political variables on expenditure measures.

Organizations also make intrastate comparisons to justify their claim for more resources. They argue that their members are slipping behind another group within the state. In Minnesota, for example, the legislature tries to keep the salaries of university faculty members pegged slightly above those of faculty members at state colleges and junior colleges. Legislators are much more sensitive to this pecking order than they are to how the university salaries compare to other Big Ten universities. Thus legislators respond to groups who make their case for additional resources in terms of how other groups are benefiting from the legislature. If intrastate justifications are indeed more persuasive than interstate ones, then political variables previously found to be unimportant for amount of expenditures might be important for share of expenditures. In fact, Salisbury offered this hypothesis years ago, but no one followed up his lead.[9]

The share of the total block-grant-action budget each state's SPA allocates to the police, corrections, and courts is investigated. Since the functional balance has changed quite a bit over the years, annual SPA grants from 1969 to 1976 are examined. In the early period when the police's share was dominant, patterns may be different from those after categorization, when the picture became more balanced. Tables 5–1 to 5–3 display the ranks of the states on functional shares in the early period, 1969 to 1972, and in a later period, 1973 to 1976. Table 5–1 displays the states' ranks on corrections share and shows considerable movement from the early time period to the later. Of the five top states in 1969 to 1972, two remained in the top five in the later period. New Hampshire dropped to twenty-second place, Utah to thirty-seventh and Massachusetts to forty-third.

Similarly, table 5–2 indicates much change over time. Of the top five states in 1969 to 1972, only New York remains at the top in the later period. Maryland and Texas moved to twenty-third and twenty-fourth, respectively, while Pennsylvania moved to twenty-sixth and New Hampshire to thirty-eighth place.

The same instability over time is evident in police allocations, shown in table 5–3. Of the top five states in 1969 to 1972, only Rhode Island remained at the top in the later period. Alabama moved to twelfth place, Wyoming to fourteenth, Nebraska to forty-fourth, and Nevada to forty-eighth. Given the amount of change over time in a function's allocation, it is appropriate to analyze the yearly allocations separately rather than to average them over time.

The growing balance among the functions in terms of allocations from the SPAs is demonstrated by the changes in the means and standard deviations of each functional share. Table 5–4 displays this information for the data. The police share has declined over the years, though not steadily. The police share actually increased over the 1969 base and, after a long period of decline, in 1975 it went up again. Both courts and corrections have been generally increasing over the years, though both lost ground in 1975 to the police. The three functional shares rarely sum to 100 because monies were allocated to other purposes besides the three functions, for example, juvenile delinquency.

The 1976 data which were coded via computer from the PROFILE system appear somewhat suspect. These data indicate that less than half the total funds were spent in the three functions, much less than in previous years. It is expected that the proportion going to the three functions together would vary from year to year but not by so much. If different patterns in the regression results occur in 1976, then these data should be ignored.

The equations are modeled individually for each of the three functions, for example, the police share is seen as a function of exchange and power-dependency strategies and the organizational strength of the police in that state. This is the formulation consistent with our theory. If the balance in allocations was being predicted on the basis of system-wide characteristics, a simultaneous-estimation technique such as path analysis might be considered. In the present theoretical formulation, however, we do not conceptualize one functional allocation as being causally related to another. Hence the allocations are estimated separately.

Table 5-1
Ranking of States on Percent SPA Allocates to Corrections, 1969 to 1972, 1973 to 1976

Rank	1969-1972	1973-1976
1	Maryland	Iowa
2	Massachusetts	Nebraska
3	Utah	Kansas
4	New Hampshire	Mississippi
5	Kansas	Maryland
6	Washington	Montana
7	New York	Virginia
8	Oregon	Pennsylvania
9	Alaska	Ohio
10	Tennessee	Louisiana
11	North Dakota	Arkansas
12	New Jersey	Wisconsin
13	Connecticut	Idaho
14	Kentucky	Nevada
15	Louisiana	Minnesota
16	Indiana	Missouri
17	Pennsylvania	Michigan
18	Illinois	Washington
19	Missouri	Kentucky
20	Mississippi	Florida
21	New Mexico	Colorado
22	Colorado	New Hampshire
23	West Virginia	New York
24	Oklahoma	West Virginia
25	Ohio	Oklahoma
26	Iowa	Tennessee
27	California	Delaware
28	Minnesota	Connecticut
29	Florida	Alaska
30	Georgia	South Dakota
31	Rhode Island	Maine
32	Arkansas	New Mexico
33	North Carolina	North Carolina
34	Michigan	Indiana
35	Alabama	Alabama
36	Idaho	South Carolina
37	Hawaii	Utah
38	South Carolina	Vermont
39	Montana	Wyoming
40	Nevada	Oregon
41	Texas	North Dakota
42	Virginia	New Jersey
43	Arizona	Massachusetts
44	South Dakota	Illinois
45	Maine	Arizona
46	Nebraska	Texas
47	Wisconsin	Hawaii
48	Vermont	Rhode Island
49	Delaware	Georgia
50	Wyoming	California

Source: Calculated by authors.

Table 5-2
Ranking of States on Percent SPA Allocates to Courts, 1969 to 1972, 1973 to 1976

Rank	1969-1972	1973-1976
1	Maryland	New York
2	New York	Vermont
3	Texas	Delaware
4	New Hampshire	New Jersey
5	Pennsylvania	Maine
6	Oklahoma	Arizona
7	Washington	Missouri
8	Wisconsin	Wisconsin
9	Louisiana	Massachusetts
10	Michigan	Nevada
11	Indiana	Kansas
12	North Dakota	South Dakota
13	Nevada	Alabama
14	Arkansas	North Carolina
15	West Virginia	Louisiana
16	Alabama	Oklahoma
17	North Carolina	North Dakota
18	Massachusetts	Indiana
19	Iowa	Illinois
20	Illinois	Connecticut
21	Missouri	Hawaii
22	Hawaii	Nebraska
23	Connecticut	Maryland
24	Georgia	Texas
25	New Mexico	Kentucky
26	Oregon	Pennsylvania
27	Minnesota	New Mexico
28	South Dakota	Iowa
29	South Carolina	South Carolina
30	Tennessee	Wyoming
31	Ohio	West Virginia
32	Alaska	Florida
33	Kentucky	Mississippi
34	Colorado	Arkansas
35	Utah	Idaho
36	Idaho	Rhode Island
37	Maine	Utah
38	Vermont	New Hampshire
39	Kansas	Washington
40	Delaware	Montana
41	New Jersey	Minnesota
42	Virginia	Georgia
43	California	Tennessee
44	Arizona	Michigan
45	Nebraska	California
46	Rhode Island	Colorado
47	Mississippi	Ohio
48	Florida	Oregon
49	Montana	Alaska
50	Wyoming	Virginia

Source: Calculated by authors.

Table 5-3
Ranking of States on Percent SPA Allocates to Police, 1969 to 1972,
1973 to 1976

Rank	1969-1972	1973-1976
1	Rhode Island	Rhode Island
2	Nebraska	Indiana
3	Wyoming	Kentucky
4	Alabama	Montana
5	Nevada	South Carolina
6	Montana	Idaho
7	Mississippi	West Virginia
8	Kansas	Georgia
9	Vermont	Arkansas
10	Tennessee	Texas
11	Virginia	Vermont
12	Connecticut	Alabama
13	Delaware	Tennessee
14	Iowa	Wyoming
15	Louisiana	New Hampshire
16	Oregon	Michigan
17	Idaho	Hawaii
18	Indiana	Oregon
19	Kentucky	New Mexico
20	New York	South Dakota
21	Arizona	Virginia
22	New Mexico	California
23	South Dakota	Illinois
24	Missouri	Louisiana
25	California	Arizona
26	Arkansas	North Carolina
27	New Jersey	Pennsylvania
28	Georgia	Oklahoma
29	West Virginia	Alaska
30	New Hampshire	New Jersey
31	Hawaii	Minnesota
32	Wisconsin	Maryland
33	North Dakota	Iowa
34	Maine	Maine
35	North Carolina	Florida
36	Florida	Washington
37	Michigan	Mississippi
38	Alaska	Utah
39	Maryland	Connecticut
40	Pennsylvania	Wisconsin
41	South Carolina	Ohio
42	Utah	Delaware
43	Massachusetts	Massachusetts
44	Colorado	Nebraska
45	Texas	Colorado
46	Oklahoma	Kansas
47	Minnesota	North Dakota
48	Washington	Nevada
49	Illinois	New York
50	Ohio	Missouri

Source: Calculated by authors.

Table 5-4
Means and Standard Deviations for Percent SPA Allocates to Police, Courts, and Corrections Functions, 1969-1976
(*percent*)

	Police		Courts		Corrections	
Year	Mean	Standard Deviation	Mean	Standard Deviation	Mean	Standard Deviation
1969	46.8	20.2	3.4	4.2	10.1	7.8
1970	62.9	12.5	5.2	3.3	12.8	7.5
1971	51.0	14.4	8.3	3.7	12.0	6.2
1972	51.3	10.0	11.0	4.8	15.1	7.1
1973	46.2	11.2	20.0	7.9	21.8	7.8
1974	36.1	16.9	23.1	9.5	26.1	12.1
1975	42.6	11.6	21.0	9.0	22.8	8.7
1976	13.5	12.2	13.9	11.6	10.8	7.2

Hypotheses for the Allocation of Resources

Proposition I asserts that organizations are influenced by the other organizations on which they are dependent. The focal organization (SPA) is more likely, then, to follow federal directives if the organizational (functional) system is dependent on federal funds of a fixed or variable nature. SPAs have received federal directives to decrease the proportion of action funds that they grant to the police. Thus, a negative relationship is anticipated between the proportion of the SPA-action budget going to police and the organizational system's dependence on block grants and discretionary funds. The state whose SPA is likely to award a low share to police is one whose total block-grant funds are a high proportion of the total state and local crime budget and whose discretionary funds are high in proportion to the population. Such a state is highly dependent on federal funding and, therefore, likely to be responsive to federal preferences.

The same congressional action that established declining funds for police as a goal also established increasing funds for courts and corrections as federal purposes. For this reason a positive relationship is predicted between the proportion of the SPA-action budget going to courts (and the proportion going to corrections) and the relative importance of block-grant funds and discretionary funds to the state. The state that is likely to award a high share of SPA funding to courts and corrections is one whose block-grant funds are relatively large and whose discretionary funds are proportionately high. Its dependency on the federal government will increase the likelihood of its compliance.

The two dimensions of state dependence are block-grant and discretionary funds, but we predict that dependence on block-grant funds is the more powerful incentive for functional allocations in accord with federal directives. Discretionary funds are limited in magnitude and directed toward limited purposes.

The block-grant funds are the "big bucks" to which we expect criminal-justice organizations to pay attention. In contrast to the importance of the exchange strategy in reaching the federal goals of innovation and system building, the power-dependency strategy is expected to be most important for functional allocations. Dollars for operating purposes are more crucial to the functional organizations than are a few dollars for innovation or coordination. Finally, it is expected that the explanatory power of the dependence equation for functional allocations will be greater than that of the exchange equation. Professional values will not be as important in channeling dollars away from police and toward courts and corrections as will dependence. Predictions about the relative power of competing explanations should also hold true for courts and corrections shares of the budget: the impact of dependence should outweigh that of exchange.

The second proposition states that the relationship between functional allocations and dependence is itself modified by the organizational strength of the function involved. Specifically, the proportion of the SPA budget going to police (reflecting the failure to follow federal directives) is negatively related to dependence and positively related to the organizational strength of the police function. To follow the federal directive is to allocate small shares to the police. This outcome is more likely in states highly dependent on federal funds and whose police possess insufficient organizational strength to overcome the effect of this dependence. High organizational strength should raise the negative slope for the relationship between the proportion of SPA funds going to police and state dependence on federal funding. Figure 5-1 shows the expected relationship. High strength is scored 1; low strength (below the median) is scored 0.

By the same logic, the proportion of the SPA budget going to courts or corrections should be positively related to dependence and strength of the courts or corrections functions. The already positive slope will be made steeper by high organizational strength in either of these functions. The overall amounts going to the functions, in contrast to amounts directed toward innovation and system building, are so large that organizations will mobilize in order to get resources for their function. When the police mobilize, this mobilization effort hinders acquiescence to federal directives; when courts or corrections personnel mobilize, their effort contributes to meeting federal directives. Organizational strength is probably a more important explanatory variable for functional allocations than for the other two dependent variables.

The third proposition is that organizations respond to the exchange of values among their personnel. Since LEAA set out to change state and local personnel through professionalization, professionals in SPAs and in state and local agencies are more likely to share the ideas of LEAA professionals about change in the criminal-justice system. We hypothesize that the following of federal directives is positively related to the level of professionalism in the SPA and the level in state and local agencies. Hence, we expect to observe a negative

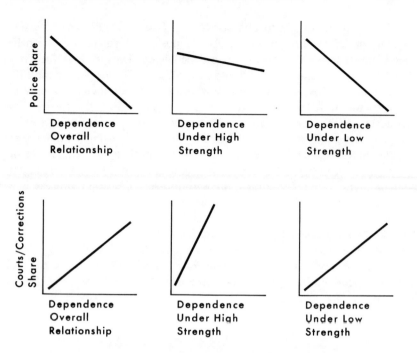

Figure 5-1. Expected Relationship between Share and Dependence under Different Conditions of Organizational Strength

relationship between the proportion of the SPA budget devoted to police (a failure to follow federal directives) and the two measures of professionalism. Similarly, a positive relationship is expected between the proportion going to courts and corrections and the two measures of professionalism. The states that are likely to give a small amount to the police and a large amount to courts and corrections are the states with highly professional SPA staffs and criminal-justice employees.

The professionalism of the SPA is expected to be more important than that of the state and local employees. It is doubtful that even a professional police employee will be supportive of his or her sector obtaining less rather than more money. Self-interest in this case would override professional concerns. On the other hand, professional SPA employees should be trying to provide more balance among functional components, whereas less professional employees might favor rewarding those with the most clout—the police—with more funds.

The fourth proposition specifies the organization's response to the inter-action of exchange and power-dependency elements in its environment. The organization's response to professionalism is believed to be much stronger under conditions of high dependence than under conditions of low dependence. We hypothesize that, for courts and corrections (where an increase indicates the following of federal directives), the already positive slope for professionalism is made stronger (more positive) by high dependence. Thus we look for a positive coefficient for the dummy variable for dependence. Figure 5-2 displays the expected relationships. For the police share (where an increase indicates the failure to follow federal directives), we hypothesize that the already negative relationship with professionalism will be made more negative or steeper by high dependence. Thus the coefficient for the dummy variable will be negative.

The federal government's dependence and exchange strategies are implemented in an environment at the state level that is already constrained by incrementalism and rational planning. In a routinized allocation process like the traditional budgetary process, it can be expected that this year's allocation will be partially determined by last year's allocation. Crime-control problems that lead to a particular pattern of functional allocations in one year are likely to exist in the next year and be met by the same pattern of allocations. Another reason for stability in a function's share from one year to the next is the renewal of projects for another year. Thus there would naturally be some carry-over

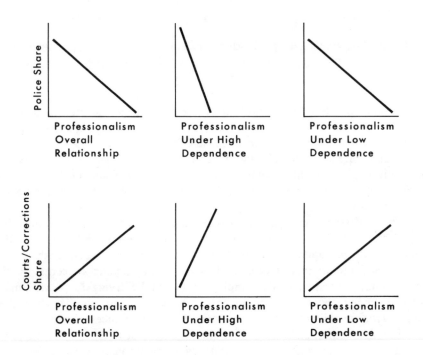

Figure 5-2. Expected Relationship between Share and Professionalism under Different Conditions of Dependence

from one year to the next in the allocations to each function. Most SPAs, however, do not allow project renewals beyond the third year. At that point, the state or local government is expected to continue the successful projects, while the unsuccessful ones will be discontinued.

In addition to incrementalism, budgetary outcomes can be explained by rationality. LEAA's planning process stresses rational decision making based on an objective assessment of the state's criminal-justice needs. This allows for state discretion in solving problems in its own way that might result in state variation from national guidelines. Yet the source of the variation is supposed to be objective differences in need for crime control, not differences in political strength of the potential recipients. Despite difficulties in measuring need for police service versus courts versus corrections, it might reasonably be expected that if rationality is an operating norm, then states with severe crime problems will exhibit similar patterns of allocation to the three functions. Patterns of allocation, therefore, will vary in accord with need. Due to lack of a theoretical literature on relative needs for different criminal justice components, more specific predictions are impossible. The desirable mix of services is unknown. We simply expect a coefficient for crime rate significantly different from zero if allocations are made on the basis of need.

Empirical Results

A number of propositions have been made predicting the police's share and a number predicting the corrections' and courts' share of SPA-action funds. The predictions are always the same for corrections and courts. These, in turn, are the opposite of the predictions for police. Though the analysis for both corrections and courts was performed, only the results for corrections are presented. Though the variance explained for courts was lower than that for corrections, the results were the same for the direction of the signs of the coefficients. The kind of relationship between variables, rather than its amount, is at the core of our theorizing. Therefore, the focus is on the signs and not the strengths of relationships.

Police

To compare the effect of the dependence strategy on police allocations with the effect of incremental and rational forces, the data presented in table 5-5 are used. Table 5-5 contains unstandardized regression estimates for equation 1, which predicts that dependence on block grants and discretionary funds will have a negative effect on the police's share if LEAA is successful in its leadership. SPAs in states that are highly dependent do not respond by reducing the

Table 5-5

Equation 1: Relationship of Police Share (*POL*) with Block-Grant Funds (*BG*), Discretionary Funds (*DF*), Crime Rate (*CRIME*), and Police Share (*POL*) at *t*–1

$POL70$ =	.587 +	.001 BG +	.122 DF –	.000 $CRIME$ +	.003 $POL69$ $R^2 = .09$
		(.002)	(.083)	(.000)	(.089)
$POL71$ =	.080 +	.002 BG* +	.043 DF +	.000 $CRIME$ +	.419 $POL70$* $R^2 = .28$
		(.001)	(.034)	(.000)	(.150)
$POL72$ =	.480 –	.000 BG –	.014 DF –	.000 $CRIME$ +	.180 $POL71$* $R^2 = .11$
		(.001)	(.031)	(.000)	(.104)
$POL73$ =	.180 +	.002 BG* –	.012 DF +	.000 $CRIME$ +	.290 $POL72$* $R^2 = .16$
		(.001)	(.024)	(.000)	(.155)
$POL74$ =	–.026 +	.005 BG* –	.133 DF +	.000 $CRIME$ +	.368 $POL73$* $R^2 = .21$
		(.002)	(.365)	(.000)	(.205)
$POL75$ =	.232 +	.002 BG +	.006 DF –	.000 $CRIME$ +	.344 $POL74$* $R^2 = .33$
		(.002)	(.016)	(.000)	(.086)
$POL76$ =	.143 +	.001 BG +	.005 DF +	.000 $CRIME$ –	.187 $POL75$ $R^2 = .04$
		(.002)	(.014)	(.000)	(.158)

*Significant at .05 level. Standard errors are in parentheses below unstandardized regression coefficients.

police share. In fact just the opposite occurs. The signs of the block-grant coefficients are nearly always positive, indicating that dependence on federal funds decreases the following of federal directives. Although the sign of the discretionary coefficient varies, it is never significant. It can be concluded, therefore, that dependence on discretionary federal funds is no more effective in producing acquiescence to federal directives than is dependence on block-grant funds.

Then what might account for the size of the police share? The SPA is planning allocations in a complex environment in which LEAA is only one actor. Rationality, rather than interorganizational struggles, may determine spending. Perhaps the process is structured to allocate funds according to need. However, the extremely small coefficients for the relationship between crime rate and police share demonstrate that critical need is not a criterion differentiating SPA allocations. Crime rate will be omitted from the subsequent analysis of police share since it has no impact on allocations.

Another possible explanation for allocation patterns among agencies is the incremental nature of any budgetary process. Evidence of incrementalism is a strong positive correlation between expenditures from one year to the next. The partial regression coefficients for the relation between two adjacent years' police shares are indeed always positive and often significant. We do not adjust for the possibility of serial correlation because the simple correlations between adjacent years are modest, ranging from –.17 to +.52, and because we are using a cross-sectional model rather than a dynamic time series model. The results are consistent with the popular view that the police were early in line for their share.

They established a baseline that was significantly larger than that of the other functions, and it was incrementally increased each year. However, it is 1970 rather than 1969 that is the big base year for the police. They increased their share from 46.8 percent in the first year to 62.9 percent in the second year. Indeed, the simple correlation between these two years is +.46, among the highest in this series. Thus the police advantage was not really established until the second year of the LEAA program. A look at the modest R^2's, ranging upward to .33, suggests that the heavy hand of the past accounts for only a part of the picture and certainly leaves plenty of room for the federal agencies to apply leverage.

Another factor that militates against a successful federal strategy is the desire of the police to receive a larger share and their organizing in support of that goal. This idea is modeled in proposition 2, comparing the best dependence variable (selected annually from the above exercise) with a dummy variable for organizational strength of the police. To conserve degrees of freedom, only one dependence variable is entered into the second equation. The dependence variable that has the largest unstandardized regression coefficient was selected. Table 5-6 presents the estimation of equation 2 with incrementalism included and need excluded. The coefficient of the dummy variable is positive (as predicted) four out of seven times, but it is never significant. Police strength, as measured, does not consistently increase the police share of SPA funds in any one year.

Table 5-6
Equation 2: Relationship of Police Share (*POL*) with Best-Dependence Measure (*BG/DF*), Interaction of Dependence and Dummy Police Strength (*INT*), and Police Share (*POL*) at *t*-1

POL70	=	.573	+ .135 (.085)	DF	- .028 (.151)	INT	- .058 (.101)	POL69	R^2 = .06
POL71	=	.131	+ .002 (.001)	BG	- .001 (.001)	INT	+ .448 (.156)	POL70*	R^2 = .25
POL72	=	.425	- .021 (.030)	DF	+ .072 (.046)	INT	+ .163 (.101)	POL71	R^2 = .12
POL73	=	.253	+ .001 (.001)	BG	+ .000 (.001)	INT	+ .268 (.151)	POL72*	R^2 = .15
POL74	=	-.076	+ .007 (.002)	BG*	- .002 (.001)	INT*	+ .440 (.195)	POL73*	R^2 = .26
POL75	=	.217	+ .002 (.001)	BG	+ .001 (.001)	INT	+ .347 (.083)	POL74*	R^2 = .34
POL76	=	.196	+ .001 (.002)	BG	+ .000 (.001)	INT	- .203 (.156)	POL75	R^2 = .04

*Significant at .05 level. Standard errors are in parentheses below unstandardized regression coefficients.

The incremental nature of the process continues to shape the SPAs' allocations in the face of police strength. The relation of this year's police share to last year's is nearly always positive and often significant. Perhaps the police have been enjoying the effects of an initial advantage that is declining over time. The progressive shrinkage in their aggregate share is consistent with this interpretation.

In the exchange strategy, the professionalism of the SPA and the police are expected to have a negative effect on the size of the police share of SPA funds. Table 5-7 reports the findings with incrementalism included. Indeed, the coeficients of SPA professionalism are rather consistently negative (with one exception), although only one is sizeable enough to be significant. But the pattern indicates that the more professional SPAs, to a modest degree, allocate less to the police than do the nonprofessional SPAs. Thus professional SPAs' actions are more in accord with federal directives than nonprofessional SPAs.

Similarly, the coefficients of police professionalism are rather consistently (with one exception) negative as expected, though significant only once. This pattern suggests that professionalism among the police is modestly related to reduced allocations to the police. The SPAs are allocating more money to the police in states with less professionalized police personnel than in states with more professionalized police personnel. This pattern is consistent with the goal of improving the criminal-justice system by strengthening its weakest subsystems. Alternately, it may be that professionalized police are less likely to use

Table 5-7

Equation 3: Relationship of Police Share (POL) with SPA Professionalism (SPA), Police-Salary Ratio (SAL), Police Share (POL) at t-1

$POL70$	=	2.157	−	.037 (.022)	SPA	−	1.522 (.540)	$SAL*$	−	.037 (.080)	$POL69*$ $R^2 = .22$
$POL71$	=	.222	−	.030 (.025)	SPA	−	.000 (.000)	SAL	+	.462 (.151)	$POL70*$ $R^2 = .23$
$POL72$	=	.525	−	.013 (.020)	SPA	−	.106 (.412)	SAL	+	.171 (.110)	$POL71$ $R^2 = .08$
$POL73$	=	.354	−	.009 (.027)	SPA	−	.051 (.135)	SAL	+	.291 (.157)	$POL72*$ $R^2 = .10$
$POL74$	=	.136	+	.042 (.032)	SPA	+	.054 (.123)	SAL	+	.376 (.213)	$POL73*$ $R^2 = .09$
$POL75$	=	.483	−	.044 (.020)	$SPA*$	−	.195 (.389)	SAL	+	.389 (.082)	$POL74*$ $R^2 = .36$
$POL76$	=	.238	−	.041 (.028)	SPA	−	.001 (.090)	SAL	−	.239 (.152)	$POL75$ $R^2 = .09$

*Significant at .05 level. Standard errors are in parentheses below unstandardized regression coefficients.

political clout to obtain SPA funds, perhaps because they are already faring so well in the state and local budgetary process.

Still, the federal exchange is working in an environment partially structured by habit. The coefficients for the relationship between the share of any two adjacent years are nearly always positive and significant in five out of seven cases. Incrementalism is usually more powerful in explaining the police share than is the exchange strategy.

Finally, the professionalism explanation is combined with the exchange explanation, while controlling for incrementalism. Table 5–8 reports findings for the combined model in which negative relationships are expected between dependence and professionalism and police share. The results are mixed. In 1971 and 1975, the direction of both relationships is as predicted: the original relationship is negative but is made more negative by the interactive term. Otherwise the relationship does not vary in a consistent fashion under different conditions of dependence. Sometimes the interaction intensifies and sometimes mitigates the original relationship. Hence it is difficult to generalize about the interaction.

The effect of incrementalism in this model is almost invariably (excepting 1976) positive. In four cases the coefficient is significant and positive. Thus the overall model demonstrates that last year's allocation generally increases next year's allocation to an important degree.

Table 5-8
Equation 4: Relationship of Police Share (*POL*) with Best-Professionalism Measure (*SPA/SAL*), Interaction of Best-Professionalism Measure and Dummy Best-Dependence Measure (*INT*), Police Share (*POL*) at *t*-1

$POL70$ = 2.620 − 2.018 SAL* + .008 INT + .028 $POL69$ $R^2 = .26$
                    (.551)   (.035)   (.082)

$POL71$ = .242 − .023 SPA − .041 INT + .415 $POL70$* $R^2 = .22$
                    (.032)   (.076)   (.171)

$POL72$ = .440 − .039 SPA + .060 INT + .139 $POL71$ $R^2 = .13$
                    (.023)   (.043)   (.105)

$POL73$ = .225 + .085 SAL + .112 INT* + .265 $POL72$* $R^2 = .16$
                    (.136)   (.060)   (.152)

$POL74$ = .117 + .141 SPA* − .154 INT* + .390 $POL73$* $R^2 = .19$
                    (.051)   (.063)   (.200)

$POL75$ = .297 − .063 SPA* − .047 INT + .381 $POL74$* $R^2 = .37$
                    (.024)   (.046)   (.082)

$POL76$ = .252 − .074 SPA* + .078 INT* − .263 $POL75$* $R^2 = .14$
                    (.030)   (.046)   (.147)

*Significant at .05 level. Standard errors are in parentheses below unstandardized regression coefficients.

What can be concluded about the ability of LEAA to move state criminal-justice systems in a certain direction—namely, toward reducing the money given to the police function? SPAs are following modestly incremental budgeting routines so that old patterns linger for quite some time. The dependence strategy does not work at all, that is, the relative size of the block-grant pie or the possibility of attracting further discretionary dollars does not appear to influence state systems. The size of the block grant is fixed by formula and does not force change.

The exchange strategy seems to be working, more so than anticipated. We thought that money (dependence) would speak louder than the complementary values of professionalism (exchange). The exchange effect is modest, to be sure, but it does exist. It highlights the importance of having planning agencies hand out funds rather than having automatic disbursals as in special revenue sharing. The SPAs do provide a mechanism for infusing federal values into a state personnel system. The positive benefits of the exchange may not outweigh its costs (that is, planning and operating funds for these agencies), but the data do not permit any such assessment.

The organizational clout of the police in acquiring funding is evident but is less important than expected. The measure may be too poor to capture their organizational strength. Alternately, their power may be systematically overrated by other observers. We tend to think that in 1969 and 1970 the police had an initial organizational advantage nationwide and therefore got the lion's share of the newly-available LEAA money. Since then, they have benefited from the incremental carry-over effect and organizational strength at the state level. In the last five years, the coefficient for police strength is positive four out of five times whereas the sign for the first two years was negative. This pattern adds weight to the argument that in recent years police strength is mobilized at the state level to counteract the overall decline in police share.

Corrections

First, the effect of the dependence strategy, incrementalism, and need are evaluated. Those results are contained in table 5-9. If the dependence strategy is working, positive coefficients can be expected for all variables in equation 1. As is evident in table 5-9, this is not the case. The coefficients describing the relationship between corrections share and dependence are about half negative and half positive. Another possibility worthy of investigation is whether the SPA is allocating money to corrections on some objective basis, such as according to the crime rate. This is not the case: the signs of the coefficients are mixed and are only significant in one case. The remaining possibility is that the allocation process is mostly incremental. Evidence for this possibility is given by the nearly always positive and frequently significant coefficients describing the relationship between adjacent years' allocations.

Table 5-9
Equation 1: Relationship of Corrections Share ($CORR$) with Block-Grant Funds (BG), Discretionary Funds (DF), Crime Rate ($CRIME$), and Corrections Share ($CORR$) at t-1

$CORR70$ =	.187 − .003 BG^* − .018 DF + .000 $CRIME$ + .224 $CORR69^*$	R^2 = .26
	(.001) (.046) (.000) (.131)	
$CORR71$ =	−.444 + .001 BG^* + .012 DF + .000 $CRIME^*$ + .631 $CORR70^*$	R^2 = .53
	(.001) (.013) (.000) (.101)	
$CORR72$ =	.048 + .001 BG^* + .012 DF + .000 $CRIME$ + .092 $CORR71$	R^2 = .09
	(.001) (.022) (.000) (.164)	
$CORR73$ =	.267 − .001 BG − .018 DF − .000 $CRIME$ + .153 $CORR72$	R^2 = .06
	(.001) (.018) (.000) (.164)	
$CORR74$ =	.321 − .003 BG^* − .271 DF^* − .000 $CRIME$ + .538 $CORR73^*$	R^2 = .22
	(.001) (.257) (.000) (.203)	
$CORR75$ =	.102 + .001 BG + .002 DF + .000 $CRIME$ + .332 $CORR74^*$	R^2 = .22
	(.113) (.013) (.000) (.096)	
$CORR76$ =	.216 − .002 BG − .017 DF^* − .000 $CRIME$ − .035 $CORR75$	R^2 = .11
	(.001) (.008) (.000) (.117)	

*Significant at .05 level. Standard errors are in parentheses below unstandardized regression coefficients.

The presence of incrementalism in police allocations was interpreted as indicative of initial police-organizational strength. In corrections allocations, how can we interpret the base of incrementalism since we earlier maintained that corrections is the organizationally weakest of the three? Seemingly, earmarking for corrections in the 1970 amendments established the baseline for corrections. Since then, incrementalism has provided a steady increase. The statistical evidence for this assertion is that the highest simple correlation between years in all three functions is for corrections in 1970 and 1971. The 1970 act increased the correctional share and carried over into the next year. The variance explained by incrementalism and the other factors is also a very respectable 53 percent in 1971.

Second, the dependence strategy is evaluated in the face of organizational strength of corrections and incrementalism. For the year 1971, the need variable is also included because it was significant in the first equation. Table 5-10 reports these findings. Corrections organizations probably would work to increase their function's share and hence the coefficient should be positive. Some tendency in this direction is evidenced, as the sign is positive five times (once significantly) and negative twice. So corrections' strength in any one year may modestly add to its share, but its share is largely determined by incrementalism—as indicated by the positive (and often significant) coefficients describing the relationship between the shares of adjacent years.

The analysis of the exchange strategy is presented in table 5-11. We anticipated positive coefficients for both measures of professionalism. Indeed, the SPA-professionalism coefficient is usually positive, though modest in size, five

Table 5-10
Equation 2: Relationship of Corrections Share (*CORR*) with Best-Dependence Measure (*BG/DF*), Interaction of Dependence and Dummy Corrections Strength (*INT*), and Corrections Share (*CORR*) at *t*-1

$CORR70 =$	$.195$	$- .003\ BG*$	$+ .000\ INT$			$+ .221\ CORR69*$	$R^2 = .24$	
		$(.001)$	$(.001)$			$(.130)$		
$CORR71 =$	$-.027$	$+ .001\ BG*$	$+ .000\ INT$	$+ .000\ CRIME*$		$+ .607\ CORR70*$	$R^2 = .52$	
		$(.001)$	$(.003)$	$(.000)$		$(.098)$		
$CORR72 =$	$.780$	$+ .114\ BG*$	$- .000\ INT$			$+ .107\ CORR71$	$R^2 = .08$	
		$(.001)$	$(.000)$			$(.178)$		
$CORR73 =$	$.198$	$- .018\ DF$	$+ .019\ INT$			$+ .137\ CORR72$	$R^2 = .05$	
		$(.017)$	$(.022)$			$(.160)$		
$CORR74 =$	$.244$	$- .004\ BG*$	$+ .001\ INT*$			$+ .588\ CORR73*$	$R^2 = .22$	
		$(.001)$	$(.001)$			$(.202)$		
$CORR75 =$	$.147$	$- .000\ BG$	$- .000\ INT$			$+ .336\ CORR74*$	$R^2 = .22$	
		$(.001)$	$(.001)$			$(.097)$		
$CORR76 =$	$.119$	$- .014\ DF*$	$+ .032\ INT$			$- .029\ CORR75$	$R^2 = .09$	
		$(.007)$	$(.025)$			$(.117)$		

*Significant at .05 level. Standard errors are in parentheses below unstandardized regression coefficients.

Table 5-11
Equation 3: Relationship of Corrections Share (*CORR*) with SPA Professionalism (*SPA*), Corrections-Salary Ratio (*SAL*), Corrections Share (*CORR*) at *t*-1

$CORR70 =$	$-.004$	$+ .021\ SPA$	$+ .116\ SAL$			$+ .249\ CORR69*$	$R^2 = .08$	
		$(.015)$	$(.153)$					
$CORR71 =$	$.022$	$- .007\ SPA$	$+ .000\ SAL$	$+ .000\ CRIME$		$+ .568\ CORR70*$	$R^2 = .49$	
		$(.011)$	$(.000)$	$(.000)$		$(.099)$		
$CORR72 =$	$.161$	$+ .002\ SPA$	$- .016\ SAL$			$+ .033\ CORR71$	$R^2 = .00$	
		$(.014)$	$(.150)$			$(.165)$		
$CORR73 =$	$.237$	$+ .011\ SPA$	$- .056\ SAL$			$+ .141\ CORR72$	$R^2 = .03$	
		$(.018)$	$(.085)$			$(.161)$		
$CORR74 =$	$.149$	$- .061\ SPA*$	$- .010\ SAL$			$+ .549\ CORR73*$	$R^2 = .26$	
		$(.021)$	$(.092)$			$(.195)$		
$CORR75 =$	$.319$	$+ .022\ SPA$	$- .204\ SAL$			$+ .385\ CORR74*$	$R^2 = .26$	
		$(.016)$	$(.200)$			$(.098)$		
$CORR76 =$	$.183$	$+ .003\ SPA$	$- .071\ SAL$			$- .036\ CORR75$	$R^2 = .03$	
		$(.016)$	$(.067)$			$(.121)$		

*Significant at .05 level. Standard errors are in parentheses below unstandardized regression coefficients.

times out of seven. Once again, as for the police, the effect of the presence of SPA professionals is to direct monies toward the achievement of federal goals. However, the coefficient for corrections-salary ratio is most often negative, contrary to our hypothesis about professionalism. This sign means that typically more funds go to corrections in states which the corrections function is less well paid than go to corrections in states in which the corrections function is better paid.

How can this pattern, already observed in the police area, be explained? Conceivably, LEAA interprets its 1970 congressional manadate to give more to corrections as directing it to improve corrections where it is weakest and its personnel are lowest paid. Hence to follow federal directives is to produce a negative coefficient. There is evidence supporting this explanation. The positive coefficients for corrections' salary ratio are in 1970 and 1971 before corrections was explicitly included in the congressional mandate; thereafter, the coefficients are negative. Thus, after the 1970 earmarking amendments, SPAs began to allocate in a totally different fashion to corrections, that is, according to need rather than according to professionalization. This pattern would be consistent with the federal goal of improving the weakest subsystems.

However, the exchange strategy is still working at a modest level in an incremental environment. The coefficients for the relationship between the shares of any two adjacent years are nearly always positive and frequently significant.

Finally, the exchange model is examined in the context of dependence as formulated in equation 4. Incrementalism is included for all years and crime rate in included for 1971. These results are reported in table 5-12. In the combined model the best professionalism variable behaves erratically. Its relationship with corrections share is sometimes positive and sometimes negative, most likely because average salary represents something more than the degree of professionalization. The interaction terms expressing the impact of different conditions of dependence are also mixed in direction. This contrary result is to be

Table 5-12
Equation 4: Relationship of Corrections Share (*CORR*) with Best-Professionalism Measure (*SPA/SAL*), Interaction of Best-Professionalism Measure and Dummy Best-Dependence Measure (*INT*), Corrections Share (*CORR*) at *t*-1

$CORR70 = .129 + .004\ SPA + .042\ INT \qquad\qquad + .201\ CORR69 \quad R^2 = .08$
$\qquad\qquad\qquad\ (.020) \qquad\quad (.041) \qquad\qquad\qquad\qquad (.146)$

$CORR71 = .001 + .000\ SAL + .001\ INT + .000\ CRIME + .601\ CORR70* \quad R^2 = .50$
$\qquad\qquad\qquad\ (.000) \qquad\quad (.001) \qquad\quad (.000) \qquad\quad (.102)$

$CORR72 = .137 + .001\ SPA - .014\ INT \qquad\qquad + .055\ CORR71 \quad R^2 = .02$
$\qquad\qquad\qquad\ (.018) \qquad\quad (.034) \qquad\qquad\qquad\qquad (.176)$

$CORR73 = .212 + .003\ SAL - .039\ INT \qquad\qquad + .125\ CORR72 \quad R^2 = .06$
$\qquad\qquad\qquad\ (.076) \qquad\quad (.031) \qquad\qquad\qquad\qquad (.159)$

$CORR74 = .164 - .130\ SPA* + .107\ INT* \qquad\qquad + .451\ CORR73* \quad R^2 = .35$
$\qquad\qquad\qquad\ (.033) \qquad\quad (.041) \qquad\qquad\qquad\qquad (.186)$

$CORR75 = .331 - .204\ SAL - .002\ INT \qquad\qquad + .337\ CORR74* \quad R^2 = .23$
$\qquad\qquad\qquad\ (.212) \qquad\quad (.024) \qquad\qquad\qquad\qquad (.094)$

$CORR76 = .177 - .066\ SAL - .001\ INT \qquad\qquad - .036\ CORR75 \quad R^2 = .03$
$\qquad\qquad\qquad\ (.066) \qquad\quad (.023) \qquad\qquad\qquad\qquad (.121)$

*Significant at the .05 level. Standard errors are in parentheses below unstandardized regression coefficients.

expected, given the mixed results in the analysis of dependence in equation 1. Dependence alone does not have a consistent impact on corrections share. Likewise its impact on the relationship between professionalism and corrections share is not consistent.

Overall, the findings for the corrections function are that the dependence strategy does not work. Its failure is probably due to the same reason that money did not create a workable dependency on the part of the police: the amount of money is simply too small. Professionalism proves to be more important than is dependence in moving corrections allocations in the direction preferred by federal policymakers. Thus SPAs are playing a modest role in directing monies toward corrections in accordance with federal directives. Additionally, the organizational strength of the corrections function often contributes to its share. These strategies are working in an environment constrained more by incrementalism than by objective need, just as in the case of the police function. In fact, incremental increases on top of the base imposed by the 1970 reauthorization may account for much of corrections' increasing share over the years.

There are indications other than the analysis of exchange and dependency strategies that LEAA is moving the criminal-justice system in the direction it desires. One test of the program's effectiveness is whether SPAs are allocating monies in the same old ways, that is, just like state and local governments' allocations. If SPA allocations funnel money to functions without considering federal directives, then the SPA allocations might be positively correlated with the percentage of the state and local budget allocated to each function in the criminal justice portion.

Table 5-13 presents the simple correlation of the two measures, percentage allocated to each function by the SPA and state and local governments. For the most part, the correlations are negative. When positive, they are quire modest. Generally, the SPAs are not making decisions on the same criteria as are the

Table 5-13
Simple-Correlation Relationship of Functional Shares Allocated by SPAs and Those Allocated by State and Local Governments

Year	Police	Corrections	Courts
1969	−.35	−.04	−.18
1970	−.26	.00	−.13
1971	−.04	−.04	.02
1972	.02	−.10	−.11
1973	.21	−.02	−.16
1974	.08	.08	−.07
1975	−.04	.03	.05
1976	−.03	.35	.07

subnational governments. The only exceptions are for police in 1969 (correlation of -.35) and for corrections in 1976 (+.35). The lack of relationship between SPA and state and local shares suggests that SPAs are resistant to many of the political forces operating at the state levels. This finding strengthens LEAA's claims that it is breaking up old patterns and forging new systems.

Another indication of LEAA's effectiveness is the progressive decline in police share of action funds. We suspect that categorization by Congress has been a big factor in reducing the police share. If categorization is responsible, it is expected that larger than average declines in police share occurred immediately after the 1970, 1973, and 1976 reauthorizations. The data already presented in table 5-4 are consistent with this hypothesis. From 1970 to 1971, police share declined by 11.9 percent and from 1973 to 1974 by 10.1 percent, the largest declines in the series except for 1976. If creeping categorization is important as a strategy, then it calls into question the continuation of the block-grant program. If LEAA as an organization can direct its target network best through categorization, then a return to categorical grants may be in order.

Notes

1. H. Brinton Milward and Gary L. Wamsley, "Policy Networks: Key Concept at a Critical Juncture" Paper presented at the Midwest Political Science Association, Chicago, Illinois, 1979, p. 31.

2. International Association of Chiefs of Police, "A Study of Police Executive Attitudes Toward LEAA," mimeographed (Gaithersburg, Md.: International Association of Chiefs of Police, 1977), Appendix 3.

3. U.S., Congress, Congressional Budget Office, *Federal Law Enforcement Assistance: Alternative Approaches* (Washington, D.C.: Government Printing Office, 1978), p. 8.

4. U.S., Congress, House, Committee on Judiciary, *Law Enforcement Assistance Administration*, 94th Cong., 2nd sess., 1976, p. 782.

5. Interview, 28 June 1978.

6. U.S., Congress, Congressional Budget Office, p. 8.

7. U.S., Congress, House, Committee on Judiciary, 1976, p. 302.

8. U.S., Congress, Congressional Budget Office, p. 8.

9. Robert H. Salisbury, "The Analysis of Public Policy: A Search for Theories and Roles," in *Political Science and Public Policy*, ed. Austin Ranney (Chicago: Markham Publishing Co., 1968), p. 165.

6 The Determinants of Innovation

This chapter's conceptual focus is innovation and its empirical focus is the states' implementation of new criminal-justice programs. Innovation in fighting crime is an important substantive goal of the LEAA program. The degree to which it is achieved, therefore, provides a standard by which to measure the effectiveness of federal strategies. Additionally, research on innovation and its diffusion constitutes an important research tradition in social science. Hence more theoretical and empirical knowledge guide the inquiry into this criminal justice area than guided the analyses of functional allocations or joint projects.

The Concept of Innovation

Innovation is an important goal of the criminal-justice block-grant program. Innovation is identified in the original act, which specifies that the state plan should "incorporate innovations and advanced techniques."[1] It is mentioned repeatedly in congressional hearings; it is seen as a goal of LEAA by the agency's outside evaluators; it is mentioned in annual reports of LEAA, and an evaluation of innovative effort is reported, as required by Congress, in the *Ninth Annual Report*.[2] Simply put, innovation is an agreed-upon goal of the Safe Streets Act and LEAA. For this reason, federal strategies of power dependency and exchange are directed in part toward its encouragement in state criminal-justice systems. Thus the explanatory factors identified by our theory should be able to explain the SPAs' commitment to innovation.

The practical definition of innovative has changed over the years, evolving from a loose definition to an increasingly strict one. A reading of congressional hearings in 1967 shows that innovation originally meant a program new to the state. The official language of the Safe Streets Act, however, equates innovation with advanced techniques, reform, and experimentation. In its reaction to the perceived inertia of state and local personnel, Congress seemed willing to try almost anything new. By 1978, however, after a decade of criticism about wasteful expenditures, Congress was requiring LEAA to demonstrate the effectiveness of innovations. Our operational definition of innovative programs incorporates the older and looser definition of innovation.

Governmental concern with innovation characterizes other policy areas and has been widely studied in political science and other disciplines. Since the pioneering work of Jack Walker in 1969 on the diffusion of innovations among states, political scientists have sought to explain variation in the adoption of new ideas.[3] A variety of political, economic, and organizational factors has been identified as determinants of innovativeness in state, urban, and national settings.[4] Whereas earlier work concentrated on identifying patterns in the relative timing of adoption, more recent work has sought to clarify the concept of innovation and be more specific about the adoption process itself.

The most theoretically sophisticated of the recent work is that of Downs and Mohr.[5] They define innovation as the earliness and the extent of use by a given organization of a given new idea. The concept *extent of use* is an advance over previous studies. In our situation where the time period of diffusion is only four to six years, relative timing is not an important dimension of innovation. Also the data show that each innovation peaked at the same time in most states so that this dimension does not exhibit much variation. Rather, the focus is on extent of use of an innovation. This is judged by the financial commitment to innovation relative to the SPA's action budget.

In studying innovation, the first operational problem is the judgment of what is new and thus innovative. Our judgment is based on a reading of the reform literature in criminal justice and talking with experts in the field about the selections. All of the programs studied were new ideas (that is, new to the nation) when LEAA started in 1969. Usually the SPA-sponsored program was the first such program in any given state, and the ideas were new to the state. Our reliance on a subjective evaluation of new and on extent of use rather than timing is consistent with Downs' practice in a recent empirical study of innovation in criminal justice. He selected deinstitutionalization in juvenile corrections (taking offenders out of penal institutions and putting them in community programs) as a new idea. He measured the extent of its use by the proportion of incarcerated offenders in community correctional programs.[6]

As already mentioned, various studies of the determinants of innovation (whether defined as timing or extent of use) have found quite a number of different explanatory factors to be important. Downs and Mohr argue convincingly that this instability of empirical findings is due to a confusion of the primary and secondary attributes of the innovation. *Primary* attributes of innovation are those that are invariant, regardless of which organization is adopting it. *Secondary* attributes vary from organization to organization (for example, relative cost). Each kind of attribute, Downs and Mohr argue, is affected by a somewhat different set of factors. In order to avoid the pitfalls of past research, separate analyses were conducted for innovations that differ on primary attributes.

We are concerned with one primary attribute: whether a given innovation is a priority of the federal government. LEAA is not simply concerned with encouraging innovation generally on the part of states but focuses on specific kinds of federally-preferred changes. How can these national priorities be identified? They are implicit in the allocation of LEAA's discretionary funds because the federal agency itself determines the national needs for which discretionary funds will be spent. In its own words, "LEAA views discretionary funds as the means to advance national priorities, draw attention to programs not emphasized in state plans, and provide special impetus for reform and experimentation."[7] Evidently, then, national priority innovations are those SPA-funded program categories which have received substantial discretionary funding. Other programs, which have been initiated by SPAs rather than by LEAA, are state priority innovations. These programs have not received substantial discretionary funding. Rather, states decided on their own to try new ideas.

Innovations Selected for Study

Six programs were selected for investigation, two from each criminal-justice function. Their characteristics are shown in table 6-1. Programs that involved most states during the period of 1969 to 1976 were selected. One program in each function had quite a bit of discretionary funding, indicating that it was a national priority, whereas three programs had relatively modest amounts of discretionary funding, indicating that they were state priorities. The extent of use or commitment to innovation is measured by the proportion of action funds (Part C or Part C plus Part E for corrections) that the SPA allocates to an innovation during this time period.

The data for each of the six measures of innovation come from a combination of computer retrieval from LEAA's PROFILE system and hand coding. For SPA action grants, computer searches on the basis of appropriate keywords were done for the 1972 to 1976 period. These projects' descriptions were then read. The final list of action grants for a particular innovation includes similar projects from one state to another. For the 1969 to 1971 period we have to rely on annual reports because PROFILE did not yet exist. Data on four of the six programs are unavailable in the early period. For organized crime and community relations, the project titles and program categories were sufficient for hand coding directly from the 1969 to 1971 annual reports. The inclusion of the early years is most important for organized crime and community relations, however, because the early years were their peak years of funding.

The coding that produced the total amount for discretionary funding (listed in table 6-1) was done in a similar fashion. For the 1969 to 1971 period, the complete listing of discretionary projects given in the LEAA annual reports was examined, and the discretionary awards to these six innovations were coded in each state. For the 1972 to 1976 period, the PROFILE system's keyword index was employed to produce an exhaustive list of discretionary grants. The grants were classified on the basis of these innovations and the amounts to each were coded.

Table 6-1
Characteristics of Innovative Programs Selected for Study

Program	Priority	Function	Amount of Discretionary Funding, 1969-1976	Percentage of Total Discretionary Funds, 1969-1976	Average Percentage of SPA Funds 1972-1976
Court management	National	Courts	$28,834,684	5.90	1.87
Public defender	State	Courts	804,982	.16	.83
Organized crime	National	Police	35,395,803	7.24	1.50[b]
Community relations	State	Police	7,416,499	1.52	1.24[b]
Community rehabilitation	National	Corrections	36,654,202	4.95[a]	1.56
Corrections training	State	Corrections	9,687,917	1.13[a]	.49[a]

[a]Percentage of Part C and Part E discretionary funds whereas other figures are proportion of Part C only.

[b]Average percentage of SPA funds is from the 1969 to 1972 period whereas other figures are for 1972 to 1976.

Courts Sector

Two innovative programs dominate the adjudicative function: court management, a national priority, and public defender programs, a state priority.

Court management involves efforts to reduce caseload, use judges' time efficiently, and rationalize the docket. These projects appear to be relatively noncontroversial and technical in nature, being supported by the American Bar Association, Congresspersons, and others who believe that "justice delayed is justice denied." The desirability of court management has been emphasized at the national level more than that of the public-defender program. Nationally, LEAA has funded some $28 million dollars worth of court management projects, devoting 5.9 percent of discretionary funds to this end. Individual SPAs came to view this movement with favor somewhat more recently than LEAA and so far have devoted only 1.87 percent of their Part C action funds toward this end. The SPAs of New Mexico and Nebraska have allocated the highest share to this program; Hawaii and West Virginia, the least.

The public-defender program, whereby the government furnishes defense counsel for the criminally-accused indigent, is quite a bit more controversial. The idea, of course, is not as new as that of court management. Public defenders are a consequence of the 1963 Supreme Court decision *Gideon* v. *Wainwright,* which rules that a lawyer must be provided for indigent-accused felons. Surveys show that prior to *Gideon* public-defender systems existed in only 3 percent of the nation's counties.[8] In the original Safe Streets legislation, Congress did not appear to include public-defender programs within the purview of the act. Senator John McClellan, in particular, worried that LEAA monies would go to the defense of criminals. Partly as a consequence of his influence, national funding by LEAA of such programs has amounted to only $804,982 or .16 percent of all discretionary funding.

State funding by SPAs has amounted to somewhat more, .83 percent. Therefore, we assume that any public-defender projects are in response to state priorities and are not an LEAA priority. In most states, providing public money to defend the accused is politically controversial. Hence, it would be expected that politically interesting variation exists in state commitment to public-defender programs. The SPAs of New Mexico and Nevada allocated the highest shares to this program. Several states (Montana, Mississippi, Alabama, Idaho, and Maine) did not allocate any money to it.

Police Sector

In the law-enforcement area two sets of innovative programs were selected: those directed at combating organized crime, and those intended to encourage improvements in police-community relations. The former was a national priority, and the latter was a state priority.

The deterrence of organized crime was clearly specified as a national priority in the original legislation. Local and state governments were ill equipped to handle criminal activity that frequently took place across governmental boundaries. In response to this incapacity, special *strike units* were established, consisting of personnel who were especially trained to fight organized crime. These specially-equipped forces consumed some $35 million of discretionary funds and were very popular in the early years of the program. On their own, SPAs allocated 1.5 percent of their monies to organized-crime units. The SPAs of Delaware and Hawaii were the most active states; Wyoming, Vermont, and North Dakota had no such activity.

In contrast, the hiring of community-relations officers was more controversial and not as uniformly adopted around the country. Community-relations units were not emphasized at the national level, as only 1.52 percent of all monies spent were allocated to such programs. State rather than national factors probably will explain commitment to community-relations programs. The SPAs of Rhode Island and New York spent the highest proportion of action funds on community-relations programs. Kentucky spent no money on such programs.

Corrections Sector

In the correctional area, community corrections is a readily identifiable innovative program which is an LEAA priority. The selection of another programmatic thrust was more difficult, but we settled on training programs for correctional personnel.

Rehabilitation in a community setting (for example, halfway houses) was a very clear national priority. Nationally, LEAA spent some $36 million in such programs, constituting 4.95 percent of the combined Part C and Part E total funds. The concept was very popular as an alternative to traditional institutions; however, its implementation was a good deal more controversial. Initially, community resistance developed to the location of halfway houses in residential neighborhoods. In more recent years the effectiveness of community rehabilitation has been debated, as its recidivism rates have been compared to those of traditional institutions. Over the course of the time period studied, SPAs varied greatly in the commitment to community corrections. Nebraska and Maryland allocated the highest share of action funds to them. Nevada, Delaware and North Dakota had no such programs.

In contrast to community corrections, training programs for correctional officers were not emphasized at the national level, receiving only 1.31 percent of the discretionary budget. Despite this lack of federal emphasis, however, they are demonstrably supported by most states. Professionalism was a later emphasis in corrections than in other functions, but little opposition arose to the concept of providing more training for employees of correctional institutions. The SPAs of Rhode Island and Alaska spent the most; several states (New Mexico, Wyoming, Idaho, Maine, and Vermont) spent nothing.

Six programs constitute the innovations which we will study in this chapter: court management, public defender, combatting organized crime, police-community relations, community rehabilitation, and training programs for correctional officers. Each of them was a new idea during the time period under study; the extent to which an SPA is committed to each innovation can be measured by the proportion of its action budget allocated to that purpose. It can be determined whether the innovation was a local or a federal initiative by observing the relative amounts of LEAA's discretionary funds devoted to it.

Interorganizational Explanation of Innovation

The propositions in chapter 2 suggest the organizational determinants of commitment to innovation. The first proposition stated that obedience to federal directives is influenced by two kinds of dependence: dependence on fixed resources represented by block-grant funds, and dependence on variable resources represented by discretionary funds. Innovation is a goal of LEAA's block-grant program, and, therefore, a general commitment to innovation constitutes following federal directives. As three of the six innovations could be regarded as national priorities, commitment of SPA resources toward these national purposes constitutes an even stronger case of following federal directives. For these reasons, we would predict that the expected positive relationships between dependence and following federal directives would be stronger (more positive) for the national-priority innovations than for the state-priority innovations.

Of these two types of dependence, it is anticipated that total discretionary funds allocated to a state (that is, variable resources) will be most important in inducing innovation because the allocation of these funds is directly tied to innovation. Indirect evidence of a positive relationship between innovation and variable dependence appears in several studies relating innovation to environmental instability and uncertainty, concepts that are similar to that of variable dependence.[9]

Fixed dependence on block-grant funds is expected to be less important in explaining innovation than in the explanation of functional allocation, although the relationship between the two should continue to be positive. The allocation of block-grant funds to the states is fixed by formula: states do not have to perform in a particular way in order to receive them. Their incentive to accede to federal demands is thereby diminished.

The second proposition in chapter 2 asserts that one organization's dependence on another rests on three factors: the amount of the resource that flows between the two, the degree to which it is critical to the recipient organization, and the degree to which the granting agency controls the conditions of its disbursal. When a high degree of dependence exists, it is likely to precipitate the mobilization of the strength of the recipient organization to influence the granting agencies. Dependent organizations are likely to mobilize their resources to seek federal funds. They are not, however, likely to mobilize in opposition to federal inducements to innovation. Thus organization-strength measures will be less strongly related to innovation than they were to variables like functional allocation. Nevertheless, high organizational strength should still depress the original relationship because some money is involved. Given the scoring of the organizational-strength variable (high = 1, low = 0), the coefficients are expected to be negative. A negative sign would indicate that high organizational strength decreases the already positive relationship between innovation and dependence (flattens the upward slope).

The third proposition in chapter 2 suggests that the degree to which agencies follow federal directives is influenced by the degree to which federal policymakers and agency personnel share professional values. Hence, because innovation is sought by LEAA professionals, its occurrence should be a positive function of the level of professionalism in the SPA and in the state criminal-justice system overall. The relationship between the likelihood of national-priority innovations and state professionalism should be even stronger (more positive) than the overall relationship. According to our argument that professionalism is the most important organizational factor in the initiation and transmission of new ideas, the exchange strategy should be more important for inducing innovation than the dependence strategy. Such a finding would not be without precedent. Other studies have demonstrated the importance of professionalism in diffusing innovations and commitment to innovation.[10] Downs found the educational level of innovating agencies to be positively related to the extent of innovation, though he did offer a caveat about this result's statistical reliability.[11] Similarly, the better-educated and presumably more professionalized state agencies will be most apt to share the innovative values of federal policymakers.

The fourth proposition in chapter 2 states that the extent of agency dependence on federal funds will modify the relationship between sharing professional values and following federal directives. The positive relationship between the amount of overall innovation and professionalism will be made stronger (more positive) by high levels of dependence. Agency dependence on federal funding gives power to LEAA policymakers. They are likely to be able to coerce compliance to their wishes if it is not voluntarily forthcoming. Shared values may suffice to produce the desired outcome. Agency dependence, however, is likely to increase the speed and enthusiasm of agencies' adoption of innovations. This heightened effect should be more pronounced for national-priority than for state-priority innovations (the coefficient for dependence will be more positive for the latter than for the former innovations).

The exchange strategy is more relevant to generating innovation than is the dependence strategy. In contrast the dependence strategy should be more important than the exchange strategy for explaining SPA's patterns of functional allocations. On the basis of these arrangements, it can be predicted that the positive relationships between dependence and innovation will be smaller than the relationships between shared values and innovation.

Drawing on the four propositions, a set of hypotheses about the determinants of innovation can be constructed. When compared to the results of other innovation studies, the findings will not result in dramatically high coefficient of multiple correlations (R^2's). They were trying to develop a total explanation for either the diffusion of or commitment to innovation. In contrast to this, we are trying to estimate the effect of organizational interactions on innovation: ours is, of course, a partial explanation.

The other elements of policymaking, incrementalism and rationality, should be mentioned as well. Incrementalism is not appropriate in this context because it is usually viewed in opposition to innovation. Annual data are not used in this chapter so it is difficult to operationalize the concept. Need, as a criterion for rational policymaking, is included, however. Need for a particular innovation should continue to be positively associated with the adoption of that innovation. Consequently, a measure of need for each innovation is developed and used in the individual (unreported) analyses. In the aggregate results reported in the next section, we use our general measure of need—crime-rate—to indicate the degree to which money for innovation is critical to solving the crime problem.

Results of the Analyses of Propositions 1 to 4

In this section, we report our results from the aggregate analysis of Propositions 1 to 4. Similar analyses were done for each of the six individual innovations to check on the presence of interesting variation by function. For two reasons, these latter analyses are not included. First, no patterns worth reporting were discovered and therefore their presentation is omitted on grounds of economy. Second, any patterns in such small programs are likely to be due to unique factors and are therefore uninformative.

Proposition 1

Proposition 1 says that an agency's propensity to follow federal directives (that is, to innovate) is positively related to the existence of two kinds of dependence on federal funding: dependence on fixed and variable resources flowing from Washington. As already argued, the variable resource of discretionary funds should be an especially important determinant of innovation. In part, discretionary funds are intended to accomplish that end. Indeed if discretionary funds do not foster innovation on the part of states, then one might question their utility. Not all innovations, however, are equally induced by such funds. When innovations are categorized as national or state priorities, discretionary monies should be more important in bringing about the latter.

Table 6–2 reports the results for the analyses of total, national-priority, and state-priority innovations. As expected, the overall explanatory power of the independent variables is low, yet the patterns confirm our expectations. Discretionary dollars have a small but significant positive effect on overall innovation. As predicted, they are especially related to the presence of national-priority innovations. The other dimension of dependence, fixed resources, does not contribute to these innovations, though its overall impact is positive as is its impact on national-priority innovations.

Table 6-2
Equation 1: Relationship of Innovation Commitment to Crime Rate (*CRIME*), Block-Grant Funds (*BG*), Discretionary Funds (*DF*)

Total	= .053	+	.000 (.000)	*CRIME*	+	.000 (.000)	*BG*	+	.004 (.002)	*DF**	$R^2 = .11$
National	= .038	−	.000 (.000)	*CRIME*	+	.000 (.000)	*BG*	+	.003 (.002)	*DF**	$R^2 = .08$
State	= .015	+	.000 (.000)	*CRIME**	−	.000 (.000)	*BG*	+	.001 (.001)	*DF*	$R^2 = .10$

*Significant at .05 level. Standard errors are in parentheses below unstandardized regression coefficients.

In examining state-priority innovations, a somewhat different explanatory pattern emerges. Obtaining relatively more discretionary or block-grant funds does not stimulate these innovations. Rather, need (as measured by crime rate) is significantly and positively related to innovation in non-national-priority areas. Thus SPAs in states with high crime rates are more likely to devote their SPA funds to these state-priority areas than are states with low crime rates. A pressing need to solve a problem does induce commitment to innovation when the state can choose the type of program. It is obvious that the state discretion offered by the block-grant concept is being exercised. The state-level factor of need explains patterns in state priorities rather than the federal strategy of power dependence.

As anticipated, the power dependence strategy has different effects in the innovation area than in the functional-allocation process. Variable dependence stimulates SPAs to follow up on innovative projects pursued by LEAA nationally. The need to "do something about crime," as measured by the state's violent crime rate, stimulates SPAs to follow up on projects initiated by states.

Proposition 2

Proposition 2 says that the influence of dependence on innovation is modified by the organization's strength within the state's organizational network. The predicted direction of the modification is negative: high strength should decrease the already positive relationship. Weak organizations are much less able to resist federal directives than stronger ones. They cannot hope for federal funding unless they please LEAA's policymakers. The coefficient of the organizational-strength dummy variable indicates if the dependence slope is significantly different among two groups: high and low organizational strength. Though organizational strength should have an effect on the relationship between innovation and dependence, the effect should not be as great as was predicted for functional allocations.

For simplicity, we chose the best measure of dependence (the largest beta coefficient), which in each case is judged to be the amount of discretionary funds received by the agency. Need was also included for state priorities due to its significance in equation one. Since the functional organizations are pressing their claims individually, the impact of each set of dummy variables is analyzed separately.

As seen in table 6-3, organizational strength does not significantly alter the original relationship between dependence and innovation. The coefficients for organizational strength differ, depending on the function. The coefficient of the dummy variable for judicial strength is negative, as predicted. In states where the judicial sector is stronger than other sectors, slightly less innovation takes place. The coefficient for the police dummy variable is positive, contrary to our

Table 6-3

Equation 2: Relationship of Innovation Commitment to Best Measure of Dependence (*DF*), Interaction of Dependence and Dummy Organizational Strength (*INT*)

Using Judicial Organizational Strength

Total	= .057	+	.007	*DF*	−	.003	*INT*				$R^2 = .11$
			(.004)			(.003)					
National	= .038	+	.004	*DF*	−	.001	*INT*				$R^2 = .08$
			(.004)			(.003)					
State	= .013	+	.003	*DF*	−	.002	*INT*	+	.000	*CRIME*	$R^2 = .12$
			(.001)			(.002)			(.000)		

Using Police Organizational Strength

Total	= .060	+	.003	*DF**	+	.002	*INT*				$R^2 = .11$
			(.002)			(.002)					
National	= .038	+	.002	*DF*	+	.002	*INT*				$R^2 = .09$
			(.001)			(.002)					
State	= .014	+	.001	*DF*	+	.000	*INT*	+	.000	*CRIME*	$R^2 = .10$
			(.001)			(.001)			(.000)		

Using Corrections Organizational Strength

Total	= .061	+	.003	*DF**	+	.002	*INT*				$R^2 = .10$
			(.002)			(.002)					
National	= .039	+	.002	*DF*	+	.002	*INT*				$R^2 = .08$
			(.001)			(.002)					
State	= .015	+	.001	*DF*	−	.000	*INT*	+	.000	*CRIME*	$R^2 = .10$
			(.001)			(.001)			(.000)		

---

*Significant at .05 level. Standard errors are in parentheses below unstandardized regression coefficients.

prediction. In states where the police are relatively strong, slightly more innovation takes place. Finally, the coefficients for the corrections dummy variable have mixed signs. If the innovations are national priorities, slightly more innovation occurs where the corrections function is stronger. If state priorities are involved, slightly less innovation occurs.

As expected, innovation is not something to which organizations organize opposition. Except for the judicial sector, there is little evidence that organizational strength reduces innovation and in that sector, the reduction is slight. Rather, innovation proceeds by the granting of discretionary federal dollars to the states. The states then fund their own innovative projects.

Proposition 3

Proposition 3 says that the degree to which states follow federal directives to innovate is a positive function of the professionalism both of the criminal-justice functions in the state and its SPA. The relationship is predicted to be stronger for national-priority innovations since they are federally induced. In table 6-4, the R^2's for the overall and state innovations are slightly higher than they were when the dependence strategy was examined. As expected, professionalism is more successful than dependence in bringing about innovation.

In contrast to our expectations, however, professionalism's impact is not significant for national-priority innovation. In further contrast to our expectations, the type of professionalism which engenders innovation is unexpected. For all kinds of innovations, the professionalism of the SPA is not significantly related to innovation. The little relation that is evident lies in the reverse direction. Instead, the overall professionalism of the state's three criminal-justice functions is positively and sometimes significantly related to overall and state-priority innovations. Neither SPA nor functional professionalism, however, is related strongly to national-priority innovations. The following of national objectives is not necessarily advanced by high levels of professionalism, but the initiation of state-priority innovations is fostered by high levels of functional professionalism. The SPA, the federal government's presence in the states, is irrelevant to these particular innovations. Instead they reflect the functional professionals' perceptions of state policy needs.

Proposition 4

Proposition 4 considers the relationship between the rate of state innovation and the extent to which shared professional values link state and federal policy-makers (that is, a successful exchange strategy exists) in the context of the

Table 6-4
Equation 3: Relationship of Innovation Commitment to SPA Professionalism
(*SPA*), Criminal-Justice Salaries (*SAL*)

Total   = .002 − .002 *SPA* + .000 *SAL** $R^2 = .12$
                 (.009)   (.000)

National = .011 − .000 *SPA* + .000 *SAL* $R^2 = .05$
                 (.007)   (.000)

State   = .009 − .002 *SPA* + .000 *SAL** + .000 *CRIME* $R^2 = .15$
                 (.003)   (.000)   (.000)

*Significant at .05 level. Standard errors are in parentheses below unstandardized regression coefficients.

extent to which states rely on federal funds (that is, a successful power-dependency strategy exists). These relationships must be analyzed simultaneously: the dependence and exchange strategies have an interactive effect on innovation. Specifically, the relationship of functional professionalism to innovation depends on the level of state dependence on variable federal resources. (The focus is on these two variables, as they are the best indicators of these two strategies' presence.) The dummy variable for high and low dependence is predicted to have a positive coefficient.

Table 6–5 displays the explanatory power of each equation. Overall functional professionalism is important in increasing total innovation. That relationship is consistently positive but varies in accord with the level of discretionary funds. The two slopes for professionalism are significantly different from one another under different conditions of dependence.

As predicted, national-priority and state-priority innovations are differently affected by this interaction. For state priorities, the slopes for functional professionalism do not differ significantly from high to low dependence. Innovation in line with national priorities, however, is significantly affected by the interaction of functional professionalism and dependence on discretionary funds. The dummy variable's coefficient is significant, showing that the response of innovation to professionalism under varying conditions of dependence is different. Seemingly, federal-state resource flows are unrelated to state-priority innovations but are important in national-priority changes. The empirical results demonstrate conclusively that exchange and dependency strategies interact to produce innovations following national goals.

Table 6-5
Equation 4: Relationship of Innovation Commitment to Best Measure of Professionalism (SAL), Interaction of Best-Professionalism Measure and Dummy Best-Dependence Measure (INT)

Total	= .007 +	.000 (.000)	SAL* +	.000 (.000)	INT*				$R^2 = .19$
National	= .011 +	.000 (.000)	SAL +	.000 (.000)	INT*				$R^2 = .17$
State	= .004 +	.000 (.000)	SAL* +	.000 (.000)	INT	+	.000 (.000)	$CRIME$	$R^2 = .14$

*Significant at .05 level. Standard errors are in parentheses below unstandardized regression coefficients.

Notes

1. U.S., *Statutes at Large,* Vol. 82, p. 201.

2. U.S., Law Enforcement Assistance Administration, *Ninth Annual Report of LEAA* (Washington, D.C.: Government Printing Office, 1978), p. 139.

3. Jack L. Walker, "The Diffusion of Innovations Among the American States," *American Political Science Review,* 63(September 1969):880–899.

4. See: Virginia Gray, "Innovation in the States: A Diffusion Study," *American Political Science Review* 67(December 1973):1174–1185; David Collier and Richard Messick "Prerequisites Versus Diffusion: Testing Alternative Explanations of Social Security Adoptions," *American Political Science Review* 69(December 1975):1299–1315; Thomas M. Scott, "The Diffusion of Urban Governmental Forms as a Case of Social Learning," *Journal of Politics* 30(November 1968):1091–1108.

5. George W. Downs, Jr., and Lawrence B. Mohr, "Conceptual Issues in the Study of Innovation," *Administrative Science Quarterly* 21(December 1976):700–714.

6. George W. Downs, Jr., *Bureaucracy, Innovation, and Public Policy* (Lexington, Mass.: Lexington Books, D.C. Heath and Co., 1976).

7. U.S., Law Enforcement Assistance Administration, *Third Annual Report of the Law Enforcement Assistance Administration, Fiscal Year 1971* (Washington, D.C.: Government Printing Office, 1971), p. 44.

8. Daniel L. Skoler, *Organizing the Non-System* (Lexington, Mass.: Lexington Books, D.C. Heath and Co., 1977), p. 179.

9. Of these, Downs' study of juvenile corrections is the most relevant to this book. He finds a .32 correlation between instability (as measured by the number of administrative reorganizations) and innovation; Downs, 1976, p. 85.

10. Richard D. Bingham, Brett W. Hawkins, John P. Frendreis, and Mary P. LeBlanc, "Professional Associations as Intermediaries in Transferring Technology to City Governments," Executive Summary for NSF (Milwaukee, Wis.: mimeo, 1978); Downs, 1976.

11. Downs, 1976, p. 101.

7

An Analysis of
System Coordination

This chapter examines coordination among different elements of the criminal-justice system, specifically joint projects that involve more than one function or governmental jurisdiction. An important goal of the Safe Streets Act is to build a criminal-justice system out of diverse and often warring elements. The analysis of coordinated activities has not been a focus of research in political science, but we can draw on sociological study of organizational interaction. The results of these studies suggest that our interorganizational theory might be useful in explaining joint ventures in criminal justice.

The Need for Coordination

One of the purposes of any block grant is the coordination of recipient agencies within a broadly defined functional area. This potential for a coordinated policy outcome is often contrasted with that of categorical programs: the latter tend to emphasize organizational differences and thereby increase the likelihood of fragmented outcomes. A number of block-grant requirements, such as comprehensive planning and broad representation on advisory boards, are aimed at promoting coordination and building linkages among previously conflicting organizations.[1] Through increasing coordination, the block-grant mechanism is intended to have a *system-building* effect.

This alleged advantage of the block grant seems to have been in the minds of the framers of the Safe Streets Act. Though the original act mentions only coordination, the later testimony of Peter Rodino clarifies the framers' intent to induce system building:

> We who framed the Omnibus Act recognized that it was hopeless to expend time and energy aimed at improving this or that aspect of law enforcement. Rather we felt that the criminal justice system as a functioning interrelationship of police, courts and correctional facilities needed coordinated planning and reform. Thus this subcommittee will be critically concerned with evaluating whether LEAA has encouraged and planned for the kind of coordination and fundamental reform that is needed, or whether it has taken the system as given and channeled resources into bolstering its power, ignoring institutional deficiencies.[2]

An examination of LEAA annual reports demonstrates that the general goals of coordination and cooperation were perceived in terms of system building. For example, the second annual report of LEAA (1970) used the word "system" three times in the first half page. On the second page under the heading "coordination," the report begins, "This entire attack upon crime is aimed at a comprehensive coordinated effort to improve the criminal justice system."[3] Operationally, system building by the SPAs at the state level occurred during LEAA's second year in the following way: "The FY 1970 plans reflected more attention to planning, training and comprehensive treatment of the criminal justice system as a system, instead of separate parts of a system. Evidence of the change is shown in regional approaches, in interdisciplinary training programs, in joint utilization of facilities and in the pooling of agencies, of approaches and of resources to make a coordinated attack on mutual problems."[4] Similarly, the recent Kennedy-Carter bill reflects a continuing congressional concern with system building. Its title is the "Justice System Improvement Act of 1978."

Outside assessments of the LEAA program also emphasize the "search for a system." The ACIR report argues that the criminal-justice program was enacted as a block grant in order to integrate the wide array of agencies at several governmental levels:

> To many, the block grant was the device best suited to facilitating communication and coordination among police departments, prosecutors, judges and corrections officials. It was anticipated that the functional component relationships within the block grant framework would eventually foster a genuine criminal justice system. "System," then, applied to police-court-corrections cooperation within individual jurisdictions as well as between cities, counties and the state. A categorical approach, in the judgment of the architects of the Safe Streets Act, would only accentuate the forces of separatism and fragmentation in the criminal justice field.[5]

The report supports the view that LEAA funds are "glue money," intended to stimulate integration in two major ways: by encouraging planning in a multifunctional body and directing action funds to support joint projects between different functions.[6]

Skoler's study of reform in criminal justice argues that the decade of 1965 to 1975 was significant for its rediscovery of "the system." He cites a number of major national study commissions, all of which stress the importance of an interrelated, interlocking criminal-justice system for dealing with the alarming rise in the crime rate.[7] Skoler's own evaluation of LEAA is reflected in his title *Organizing the Non-System*. Despite all attempts, he believes that unification of the diverse elements has not yet been achieved.

In summary, system building—more specifically, functional and jurisdictional coordination—is a goal of any block grant. It is recognized as a goal of the Safe Streets Act by congresspersons and by LEAA. Despite this consensus about the goal, outside evaluators view it as only partially realized. Our understanding of the degree to which LEAA has succeeded in its realization, however, is far from complete. The topic's importance mandates continued research on the problems of and prospects for interorganizational and intergovernmental cooperation.

One of the most important statements on coordination is Pfeffer's and Salancik's. They conceptualize coordination as a way of reducing uncertainty in an organization's exchange with its environment.[8] They consider several types of coordinating mechanisms—social norms, cooptation, cartels, and joint ventures. The *joint venture* is most similar to the cross-system projects that will be examined, as it refers to two or more organizations joining together to create a new organization or subsidiary. In an earlier study, Aiken and Hage focused on the related phenomenon of joint programs between organizations—a kind of organizational interdependence established for the purpose of acquiring additional resources.[9] The *joint program* is even more similar than the joint venture to our measure of intrasystemic coordination because the joint program is not a new entity like the latter but a more temporary, one-shot project.

The reformers' goal of building a coordinated criminal-justice system is the goal of creating rational organizational interdependence, similar to that studied by Pfeffer and Salancik and Aiken and Hage. Accordingly, the conditions under which criminal-justice functional organizations in the states seek to establish such interdependence will be assessed. The conditions within the organizational system that foster coordination will be analyzed, as well as the strategies by which the federal government seeks to increase coordination. The propositions from the interorganizational theory can be used to generate hypotheses that predict these conditions.

The Measurement of Coordination

Consistent with the studies cited above, *coordination* is conceived of as evidenced by joint projects carried out by more than one criminal-justice function or jurisdiction. Some examples of such joint projects funded by SPAs are: criminal-justice information systems which service all three functions; Youth Services bureaus which combine police and courts functions; Youth Advocates which combine the courts and corrections functions.

Two possible kinds of data exist that might accurately measure joint activities. One describes projects that affect more than one function, and the other catalogues projects that involve coordination. Selection of the latter designation produces a rather small universe of projects, which may include coordination among governmental jurisdictions as well as among functions. The word "coordination" has to appear in the project description in order for it to be included in the census, ensuring that the coordination is conscious and mutually perceived.

A study of projects that affect more than one function would have the advantages of being restricted to functional interactions and offering a larger number of projects to analyze. However, it has the distinct disadvantage that the involved organizations may not necessarily be coordinating their activities. A project may be coded as *joint* because one organization perceives that its actions have an effect on another organization. This effect might be unrecognized or unwanted by the second organization. Any list of "projects affecting more than one function," therefore, probably overestimates the amount of coordination, while a catalogue of "projects involving coordination" underestimates the amount of coordination. In such a case, the conservative decision is to use the latter indicator of coordination.

A final measurement decision was whether to use the number of joint projects or the amount of money (either absolute or relative) devoted to joint projects as the indicator of coordination. Some analysis of both measures was done, but the total amounts of money involved were so small that their analysis was not very useful. Finally, the same measure used by Pfeffer and Salancik and Aiken and Hage was adopted: the number of joint projects. We feared that the number of joint projects might be simply a function of the total number of projects funded by the SPA because states vary greatly in the numbers of projects they fund. Alternately, it could be a function of the number of criminal-justice agencies in the state. Neither of these variables, however, was correlated with the number of joint projects.

Data were obtained for two years, 1973 and 1976, in order to examine the growth in coordination over the years. The earliest date for which reliable data are available is 1973, and 1976 is the latest year for which all the reports are recorded. These data were obtained from the PROFILE system, LEAA's computer-based information system, with the assistance of the National Institute of Law Enforcement and Criminal Justice. States in the earlier year averaged 5.10 coordinated projects. In 1976 states showed a modest increase to an average of 6.55 projects involving coordination.

The projects studied are all funded by the SPA with block-grant-action funds, and are intended to be used, in part, to build a cooperative and coordinated criminal-justice system.

An Interorganizational Explanation of Coordination

Coordination is the planned and self-conscious interdependence of two or more organizations. Coordination of functional and jurisdictional elements is an agreed-upon goal of the Safe Streets Act. The number of joint projects, therefore, is a measure of the system coordination sought by policymakers. With some respecification, the propositions developed in chapter 2 yield hypotheses about the conditions under which the power-dependency and exchange strategies produce coordination among functions. These hypotheses, however, should be analyzed along with the explanation of rationality as a determinant of coordination. A measure of need for a coordinated attack on crime (that is, violent-crime rate) is available and can be used to evaluate the rationality of coordination.

Proposition 1 asserts that organizations are influenced by two kinds of dependencies: fixed and variable. Organizations within relatively dependent organizational systems are more likely to cooperate with one another than are organizations within relatively independent systems. If the organizational system depends heavily on the federal government, the organizational system will follow the federal directive to become more coordinated. Coordination is induced by federal control over a significant proportion of state criminal-justice funds. Consequently, positive relationships are expected between the two measures of dependence and the number of joint projects.

Yet dependence probably will not be as important an explanatory concept for joint projects as it was for functional allocations. Dependence on federal funds motivates organizations to seek LEAA's money but does not necessarily motivate organizations to follow federal directives to be innovative or cooperative. The exchange strategy, in comparison with the dependence strategy, may be more effective in fostering joint ventures among organizations. The dependence strategy is based on state organizations' need for federal monies. Dependent states are assumed to be relatively powerless to resist federal demands. In contrast, the exchange strategy is noncoercive: shared values between federal and state policymakers are assumed to lead to shared policy preferences. Professionalism alters the priorities of state policymakers. Rather than attempting to maximize the agency's budget, they attempt to maximize professional values. In explaining joint ventures, the expected R^2's for the dependence equation will be lower than the R^2 for the exchange equation.

Of the two dimensions of dependence, variable dependence is expected to be the most effective in bringing about coordination among functional elements. These discretionary funds are aimed at attaining national goals such as innovation and system building. Their allocation can be changed easily by LEAA. We predict that the relationship between joint projects and discretionary funds will be stronger (more positive) than the relationship between joint projects and block-grant funds. Block-grant funds are not readily manipulatable by LEAA and cannot be used to reward "obedient" state agencies and punish "disobedient" ones. Extant empirical literature provides little guidance for this proposition. Aiken and Hage, whose research comes closest to dealing with this issue, do not test their central thesis that the need for resources drives organizations to coordinate.

Finally, a positive relationship is anticipated between the number of joint projects and the crime rate. States with critical crime problems will seek to solve that problem through any means possible, including coordination of the attack of police, courts, and corrections. The assumption is that a coordinated system is better able to combat crime. Therefore, there is an incentive for planners, beset by a severe crime problem, to encourage coordination.

The second proposition asserts that the degree of state responsiveness to dependence on the federal government is modified by the strength of organizations within the state. The strength of organizations, then, should affect the likelihood that they will coordinate their activities. The theoretical argument of Pfeffer and Salancik is clear: organizations coordinate to stabilize uncertainties stemming from environmental dependencies. Their own empirical studies furnish less guidance about how to measure or model the condition of uncertainty. In situations of intermediate concentration, they hypothesize that organizational environments are more uncertain than in situations of either high concentration (only two industries) or low concentration (many small industries).[10] Consequently, organizations will be more likely to coordinate in environments of intermediate than of high or low concentration. Further, Pfeffer and Salancik argue that coordination is a function of the feasibility of interfirm linkages. Joint projects are more likely where only a few organizations are present. In general, coordination is readily attained when the number of relevant actors is small; when the number is very small, however, it is unnecessary.

A *concentration ratio* measures the share of the market possessed by the top few firms in an industry. In the analysis of a business firm's propensities for joint projects, this ratio would be crucial. This measure is not applicable to this situation. The same three industries (police, courts, corrections) are present in all states. Also we are analyzing the cooperation of one organizational system with another at the state level (that is, police-court cooperation), whereas other studies analyzed the cooperation of one particular organization with another (why one particular policy agency cooperates with a court).

Unable to replicate directly other scholars' indicators of propensity to coordinate, their logic about the necessity for and feasibility of coordination was considered. The analysis of industries presumes that, regardless of the number of firms, they are all relatively equal in strength. In a market, inequality of strength quickly leads to the destruction of the weak by the strong. The important variable is the number, not the relative power, of organizations in a system. In the nonmarket organizational system of criminal justice, however, the situation is reversed. Any such system has approximately the same number of actors; their relative power, however, varies widely. The indicator of propensity to coordinate, therefore, should focus on the equality of organizational power and not on the number of organizational actors.

Seemingly, members of organizational systems are more likely to coordinate their activities when they are relatively equal in strength. Great inequality of power permits powerful actors to ignore less powerful ones. The former affect the latter, but the reverse is not true. The weaker organizations are likely to be highly motivated to coordinate with the stronger, but no incentive exists for the larger ones' cooperation. Little coordination is likely to occur in such a system. In contrast, when organizations are equally powerful, they are equally motivated to seek coordination as a means of minimizing uncertainties due to others' actions.

We experimented quite a bit with various measures of equality of organizational systems (police, courts, and corrections) within each state. The measure we settled on is computed in the following way. First, the absolute pairwise differences in the organizational strength index, introduced in chapter 4, was computed. Police were compared with corrections, police with courts, and courts with corrections. Then the sum of those absolute differences was computed for each state. A high score reflects large differences among the organizational strengths of the functions in that state (*inequality*) and a low score reflects small differences among the functions (*equality*).

These scores for 1973 are displayed in table 7-1. Alaska is the state whose criminal-justice functions vary most in their organizational strengths, followed by the smaller states of Vermont, North Dakota, and Hawaii. Iowa is the state

Table 7-1
Rank of States on Sum of Absolute Differences in Organizational Strength, 1973

Rank	State	Rank	State
1	Alaska	26	Nebraska
2	Vermont	27	Maine
3	North Dakota	28	Missouri
4	Hawaii	29	Indiana
5	Illinois	30	Massachusetts
6	Colorado	31	Florida
7	Georgia	32	Wyoming
8	South Carolina	33	Connecticut
9	North Carolina	34	Virginia
10	Maryland	35	Texas
11	Rhode Island	36	Montana
12	Kansas	37	Nevada
13	Mississippi	38	New Mexico
14	Delaware	39	Ohio
15	Oregon	40	Michigan
16	New York	41	Tennessee
17	Arkansas	42	Utah
18	California	43	Pennsylvania
19	Wisconsin	44	Minnesota
20	Alabama	45	South Dakota
21	New Jersey	46	Oklahoma
22	Washington	47	Idaho
23	Kentucky	48	Louisiana
24	Arizona	49	West Virginia
25	New Hampshire	50	Iowa

whose functions are most equal on this dimension, and consequently it is expected that Iowa's criminal-justice functions undertake more joint projects than Alaska's.

This variable is then transformed into a dummy variable. States with large differences (above the median) take on the value of 1. States with small differences (below the median) take on the value of 0. Given this scoring of the dummy variable and the assertion that equals tend to cooperate, a negative coefficient for the dummy variable is predicted. The positive relationship between dependence and joint activities will be less strong (flatter) when organizations are unequal (coded as 1). Because of the lack of prior empirical research at the systemic level, this hypothesis is more tentative than others that have been proffered.

The third proposition in chapter 2 considers the effect of shared values held by decision makers in different organizations. Such shared values are likely to lead to similar priorities and policy preferences. LEAA is staffed with professionals, and its policy objectives are presented as being professionalized. State-level criminal-justice professionals probably will be likely to agree with LEAA's diagnosis of necessary actions. Accordingly, SPAs and criminal-justice functions with more professionalized staffs will tend to follow the federal directive of coordinating the criminal-justice system. The relationship between joint projects and the two measures of professionalism will be positive. Some support for this prediction exists in the empirical literature. Aiken and Hage discovered a positive association between two measures of professionalism and the number of joint programs.[11]

The fourth proposition in chapter 2 says that organizations respond to the interaction of exchange and dependence. More specifically, the likelihood that an organization will follow federal directives is increased by professionalism, and further increased by dependence on federal funds. The positive impact of professionalism is likely to be much more pronounced when money in either large or variable amounts is involved. When a dummy variable expressing high or low dependence is incorporated into the predictive equation, the positive relationship between coordination and professionalism will be stronger (more positive) under conditions of high dependence.

Empirical Results for Joint Projects, 1973 and 1976

Proposition 1 states that the number of joint projects is a positive function of dependence. It is modeled by the now-familiar equation One, presented in table 7-2. The results are quite unexpected. In 1973 all coefficients are unexpectedly negative, although only one is significantly so. In 1976 the signs are still negative for the relationship of the number of joint projects to the two dependence variables, significantly so for discretionary funds. In 1976, however, the crime

Table 7-2

**Equation 1: Relationship of Number of Joint Projects with Crime Rate (*CRIME*),
Block-Grant Funds (*BG*), and Discretionary Funds (*DF*)**

Joint 73	=	12.673	−	.098 (.038)	*BG**	−	1.460 (.960)	*DF*	−	.002 (.005)	*CRIME*	$R^2 = .16$
Joint 76	=	6.381	−	48.151 (83.398)	*BG*	−	.802 (.290)	*DF**	+	.014 (.006)	*CRIME**	$R^2 = .25$

*Significant at .05 level. Standard errors are in parentheses below unstandardized regression coefficients.

rate is significantly positive in its relationship to the number of joint projects, as predicted. In 1973 states that received very little in the way of block-grant funds were more likely to coordinate at the agency level. In 1976 states with high crime rates and states receiving few discretionary dollars were likely to coordinate among functional elements.

How can we explain this unanticipated consequence? The significance of the coefficients demonstrates that the unexpected results are not merely reflecting random events. The most straightforward interpretation is that coordination takes place regardless (perhaps in spite of) of any federal strategy of power dependency. In this interpretation, the frequency of joint projects is a function of factors that include the state's need, as indicated by a high crime rate. Federal funds fixed by formula do not stimulate system building. Only the necessity for system building generates it. An alternative interpretation credits federal policymakers with more tactical sense. It suggests that federal discretionary funds are being allocated to the states with the least coordination in an attempt to improve that lack. Hence, there is a negative sign for the discretionary coefient in both years. Both interpretations, however, conclude that federal monies have not strikingly increased intrastate coordination.

The second proposition incorporates the degree of intrastate organizational equality into the consideration of the effect of the federal-dependence strategy. This proposition was derived from studies of coordination among firms. The strongest dependence variable (block-grant funds for 1973 and discretionary funds for 1976) was selected and their interaction with the dummy variable for systemic inequality was examined. Crime rate is included for the 1976 equation because of its significance in the first equation.

The results for equation Two are shown in table 7-3. The differences in organizational equality do not matter. In both 1973 and 1976 the coefficients of the dummy variable are not significant. Despite the differences in the signs, coefficients have to be considered as zero. In each year, an important and significant factor in explaining coordination is the degree of dependence on

Table 7-3
Equation 2: Relationship of Joint Projects with Best Measure of Dependence
(*BG/DF*), Interaction of Dependence and Dummy for Inequality of Organi-
zations (*INT*)

Joint 73 = 10.086 − .071 *BG** − .018 *INT* $R^2 = .14$
                          (.031)   (.019)

Joint 76 = 3.793 − .819 *DF** + .142 *INT* + .015 *CRIME** $R^2 = .24$
                          (.337)   (.005)

*Significant at .05 level. Standard errors are in parentheses below unstandardized regression coefficients.

federal funds. The impact of dependence, however, is opposite to the original hypothesis: high dependence leads to less coordination. The results also show that in 1976 the crime rate continued as a significant factor in fostering coordination. States with severe crime problems have more coordination among different elements of the criminal-justice system than states with lesser crime problems.

Organizational strength, as measured here, is not important in explaining coordination. Since the theoretical formulation of this part of the proposition was shaky, counterarguments must be examined for the unexpected finding. First, we may not have the most appropriate measure of the organizational conditions that foster coordination. Several variations were tried on the basic measure presented here but without different results. Second, organizational strength's effect may be most appropriately modeled in a different fashion. We tried adding the dummy variable and letting only the intercept vary but the explained variance and signs of the coefficient were the same. Third, it is likely that the problem is a level-of-analysis problem: differences in the equality of organizational systems (which are measured here) may not influence an agency's decision to enter into a joint project with an agency from another function. The latter decision is captured by micro level measures of organizational equality that others have used in their research. Our data do not inform us as to the equality of the hundreds of criminal-justice agencies in each state.

The third proposition asserts that the likelihood of coordination is increased by the presence of a professional-exchange relationship. The results for equation Three are reported in table 7-4. The coefficients are generally positive as predicted but only one is significant. The level of SPA professionalism has a positive effect on coordination in both years. Professionalized SPAs fund more coordinated projects than do less professionalized SPAs. The fact that the relationship is stronger in 1976 suggests that SPAs are increasing their efforts to build a criminal-justice system out of diverse elements.

Professionalism among criminal-justice-system employees has little effect on

Table 7-4

Equation 3: Relationship of Joint Projects with SPA Professionalism (*SPA*) and Criminal-Justice Salaries (*SAL*)

Joint 73 =	.557 +	1.193 (1.070)	*SPA* +	.006 (.006)	*SAL*				$R^2 = .12$
Joint 76 =	4.504 +	3.137 (1.481)	*SPA** −	.001 (.006)	*SAL* +	.009 (.006)	*CRIME*	$R^2 = .21$

*Significant at .05 level. Standard errors are in parentheses below unstandardized regression coefficients.

coordination. In 1973 the indicator of their professionalism is positively related to the number of joint projects and in 1976 it is negatively related. Neither funding, however, can be regarded as significantly different from zero. The severity of the crime problem continues to exhibit a slight positive relationship with the degree of intrasystemic coordination in 1976.

We had hypothesized that professionalism would be more important than dependence in facilitating coordination. In fact, SPA professionalism exerts a positive influence on coordination while dependence exerts a negative influence on coordination. Professionals are achieving a more coordinated criminal-justice system even though fund flows from LEAA are not effectively structured to induce such coordination. To the extent that any system building is occurring, it is due to the exchange rather than the dependence strategy.

The fourth proposition allows us to investigate the effect of the two federal strategies simultaneously. Equation 4 combines the best measure of the existence of a dependence relationship as a dummy variable with the best measure of the existence of an exchange relationship (SPA professional score for both years). In 1976 the crime rate is also considered. Table 7-5 reports the results. For the first time differences were discovered between the model in which the dummy variable altered the slope and the model in which the intercept

Table 7-5

Equation 4: Relationship of Joint Projects with Best Measure of Dependence (*SPA*) and Dummy Best Measure of Professionalism (*INT*)

Joint 73 =	5.324 +	1.406 (1.109)	*SPA* +	1.399 (2.018)	*INT*				$R^2 = .10$
Joint 76 =	3.181 +	3.761 (1.560)	*SPA** −	2.338 (2.683)	*INT* +	.009 (.006)	*CRIME*	$R^2 = .22$

Significant at .05 level. Standard errors are in parentheses below unstandardized regression coefficients.

varied. The intercept varying equations had slightly higher R^2's but the coefficients are similar. Since we are concentrating on the latter, discussion of the intercept model is omitted.

The impact of dependence is negligible. In the earlier year the interactive term slightly increased coordination. In the later year it slightly decreased coordination. The impact of SPA professionalism on intrastate coordination continues to be positive for both yeas. In 1976 its coefficient is significant. When the exchange and dependence strategies are implemented in combination, exchange dominates. The 1976 crime rate continues to have a slight positive relationship with joint projects but the coefficient is not significant. The consideration of objective needs does not furnish much incentive to coordinate.

In the early period, neither federal strategy significantly changes an organizational system's propensity to undertake joint projects with another system. By 1976, the responsiveness of system building to the exchange strategy was evident, though the number of joint projects were decreased by the separate effect of discretionary fund flow. The original hypothesis to the effect that exchange would prove to be more important than dependence for system coordination is upheld for 1976.

Conclusion

In both 1973 and 1976, the two years examined, the average number of joint projects involving coordination was low. Given the infrequency of the occurrence of coordination, perhaps it is not surprising that our theory falls somewhat short in explaining much of the variation from one state to another. Much of the initiative in coordination lies within the individual agencies, and external attempts to speed up coordination are limited in their ability to affect internal agency decisions. Even if a more generous measure of coordination had been used and projects affecting more than one function were focused on, the number of joint projects would still be low: 18.7 was the mean for 1973 and 24.0 for 1976. Apparently, few system-building efforts have been undertaken and the frequency of such efforts has not increased much over time.

A comparison of system building with innovation and functional allocation suggests why system building is lagging. If we look at 1976, there are some differences in the conditions under which the goals of innovation and coordination are accomplished. We assumed that the achievement of both goals would be more heavily influenced by professionalism than by state dependence on federal funding. In all cases, professionalism was important. In each instance, however, discretionary or targeted funds were more influential than fixed funds—but targeted funds increased innovation while they decreased coordination. Apparently the stated purpose of discretionary programs, to encourage experimentation, is precisely to encourage innovation and not system building.

The role of the oft-criticized SPA is crucial in the stimulation of coordination. If joint projects are left to the discretion of the criminal-justice functional components, they would evidently occur even less frequently than they do now. Functional components will innovate on their own, without SPAs' encouragement. In contrast, they need some stimulus to coordinate their activities. The relative political strengths of the functional components within the state is irrelevant to the achievement of either the goal of innovation or coordination. When the number of innovative or coordinated projects is small, state organizational systems are not mobilizing their strength to capture that process. When the number and monetary worth of these projects increase, the situation may change.

If much coordination is to occur, however, something more than the exchange strategy is needed. Apparently, professional values are not a strong impetus to the cumbersome task of interorganizational coordination. In the case of functional allocations, earmarking achieved balance among the functions. The carrot-and-stick approach to inducing compliance to federal directives is often effective. To achieve intrasystemic coordination, Congress could require that a certain percentage of LEAA funds go to projects carried out by more than one function or jurisdiction. Without such an action, system building is likely to remain a distant goal.

Notes

1. Carl W. Stenberg, "Block Grants in Transition: The Politics of Categorization and Recategorization" (Paper for the American Political Science Association, Washington, D.C., September 1977), p. 9.

2. U.S., Congress, House, Committee on Judiciary, *Law Enforcement Assistance Administration,* 93rd Cong., 1st sess., 1973, p. 2.

3. U.S. Law Enforcement Assistance Administration, *Second Annual Report of the Law Enforcement Assistance Administration, Fiscal Year 1970* (Washington, D.C.: Government Printing Office, 1970), p. 2.

4. Ibid., p. 4.

5. U.S., Advisory Commission on Intergovernmental Relations, *Safe Streets Reconsidered: The Block Grant Experience, 1968–1975* (Washington, D.C.: Government Printing Office, 1977), p. 180.

6. Ibid., p. 181.

7. Daniel L. Skoler, *Organizing the Non-System* (Lexington, Mass.: Lexington Books, D.C. Heath and Co., 1977), p. 18.

8. Jeffrey Pfeffer and Gerald R. Salancik, *The External Control of Organizations* (New York: Harper and Row, 1978), pp. 143–145.

9. Michael Aiken and Jerald Hage, "Organizational Interdependence and Intra-organizational Structure," *American Sociological Review* 33(December 1968):912–931.

10. Pfeffer and Salancik, 1978, p. 155.

11. Aiken and Hage, 1968, pp. 920–921.

8   Conclusion

There are two strategies available to LEAA in its attempts to influence state and local criminal-justice agencies. One strategy, labeled power-dependence, involves controlling the federal funds flowing to state and local agencies. However, the amount of money controlled by LEAA is small and the degree of control exercised over this money is limited. The second strategy, the exchange strategy, involves controlling the decision premises of state and local policymakers. Although there is evidence that exchange has worked better for LEAA than power dependence, the conditions for a successful exchange strategy are only rarely met by the agency.

Interorganizational Theory and the Law Enforcement Assistance Administration

This book has examined LEAA's ability to influence state and local criminal-justice agencies in the pursuit of three specific goals: more balanced allocation of funds among criminal-justice functions, increased innovation, and systems building or increased coordination between criminal-justice functions. The agency's actions vary widely in the degree to which they are effective in moving states toward these goals. Its most successful actions involve either reliance on exchange in combination with power-dependence strategies or exchange alone. Overall, however, there is little evidence of well-planned tactical use of these strategies by federal policymakers.

Recapitulation of the Data Analysis

In the attempt to achieve greater parity among criminal-justice functions, LEAA has been only moderately successful. Over the period of the research for this book, SPAs have ceased allocating the lion's share of block-grant funds to police. This trend, however, is not much influenced by the amount of either fixed block-grant funds or discretionary funds flowing into the state. This lack of effect is attributable to the facts that these funds are a small percentage of state and local criminal-justice budgets and, further, that they are not readily controllable by LEAA. Therefore, block-grant funds fail to create power-dependence relationships between LEAA and state and local agencies.

The explanation for the actual pattern of allocation of funds among functions involved three factors. First and foremost, incrementalism is a fairly powerful explanation. In general, the percentage of funds flowing to a given function was influenced by the percentage that function received the previous year. Although this is not an unprecedented finding, it is surprising that incrementalism was not the singularly dominating factor it is usually found to be in studies of public policy. Allocation patterns changed dramatically during some periods despite this tendency toward predictable change. To be sure, initial patterns of resources' commitment were significant determinants of later patterns of resource investment. The police function was the best organized of the three functions, and its representatives were first in line when block-grant programs were started. Thus they secured for themselves a large initial piece of the block-grant pie. This share, however, steadily declined in most years and dramatically declined in a few years. The iron grip of the past is not quite as strong in the allocation of the block-grant funds by SPAs as it is in other areas of public policy.

This finding is encouraging: SPA decision makers have demonstrated an ability not found in other areas of public policymaking—to reevaluate and then alter the allocation of funds at their disposal. This evident flexibility suggests that LEAA is not locked into a pattern of resource distribution that can only be changed at the margins. Under certain conditions, therefore, changes in policy and priorities can be swiftly translated into changes in the allocation of block-grant funds. Such change, of course, depends on LEAA's influence on the SPAs' shifting of their allocational patterns.

Where the impact of incrementalism was weak, two other factors affected the allocation of funds. Earmarking of funds by Congress had a significant effect, altering the flow of block-grant funds to the criminal-justice functions. Categorization of funds, however, did not merely disrupt the incrementally changing patterns of the past. It established new patterns that were institutionalized and developed incrementally. By guaranteeing a share of the block-grant pie, earmarking provided a base from which the corrections function, for example, was able to expand in an incremental fashion.

Finally, the professionalism of the SPAs affected their allocations of block-grant funds. This has been referred to as the exchange strategy of federal influence because it seeks to use the prestige of the professionalized agency to induce voluntary cooperation in the achievement of federal goals. Professionalized SPAs, as predicted, tended to allocate a smaller percentage to the police and a higher share to the other two functions than less professionalized agencies. In general, our research provides evidence of the success of this strategy: actual federal influence was more a result of the sharing of professional values between state and federal policymakers (the exchange strategy) than a result of the influence of levels of either fixed or discretionary block-grant funds (power-dependence strategy). These results indicated that in practice the exchange strategy was more successful than the power-dependence strategy. This success was, however, only relative and achieved only under certain conditions.

In the analysis of variations in commitment to innovation, the flow of federal dollars into a state was not a significant explanatory factor. This results from the generally small amount of money at stake and the difficulties involved in controlling its flow. Instead, we found that the professionalism of personnel in a criminal-justice function was the best single predictor of commitment to innovations in that function. Significantly, functional professionalism and not SPA professionalism is important. The state's priorities determined the innovations to which these professionals tended to be committed and not the priorities of LEAA at the federal level.

This finding provides several insights into the dynamics of the exchange strategy and the difficulties involved in achieving specific federal goals via exchange alone. The essence of the strategy is to turn local decision makers into people who share values and interests with federal decision makers. Even when this convergence of interests is achieved, however, the strategy can still lead to policy outputs different than those desired by federal policy makers. Professionals, with shared values but situated in different contexts, may respond to different types of influences and thus produce different policies. In the analysis of commitment to innovation SPA professionals respond to LEAA, while functional professionals are more responsive to the particular needs of the states within which they are located.

The measure of need—state-per-capita—crime rate—was significantly associated with commitment to state-priority innovations. Those states with high levels of need tended to spend more on innovations. This finding, coupled with the importance of functional professionalism, is important. It may be used to justify increasing the autonomy of state-level policymakers. Professionals within state and local criminal-justice agencies may be closer to the specific needs of their areas than are either federal-level personnel or SPA staff members. In interviews with representatives of interest groups representing the three criminal-justice functions, respondents expressed the belief that the SPA planners never really understood the specific needs of the states within which they operated. Such a belief may be more than predictable interagency animosity or local-level resentment of federal meddling. It may be an accurate perception of the problems inherent in centralized policymaking. As our findings corroborate this belief, they suggest that if meeting states' needs is the intent of block grants, decisions may often be made best by personnel in line criminal-justice agencies. When these local criminal-justice personnel adhere to professional norms, they may be the most appropriate decision makers.

Finally, the analysis of innovation points to an interaction between discretionary funding and SPA professionalism in the case of national-priority innovations. States with high levels of SPA professionalism and discretionary funding tended to spend more on national-priority innovations than states with just high professionalism or high discretionary funding. If LEAA seeks commitment to national-priority innovations, it must successfully combine power-dependence and exchange strategies. Given the propensity of functional professionals to spend money on state-priority innovations, the implementation of a single strategy (either exchange or power-dependence) is unlikely to result in actions reflecting national priorities.

Analysis of coordination between criminal-justice functions provides little evidence of successful achievement of LEAA's system-building goal. Overall, LEAA did not have much of an impact on the states. The limited impact that it did have, however, was through shared values of personnel rather than control over block-grant funds. This result indicates that exchange—here induced by SPA professionalism—was more effective than power dependence in influencing state and local criminal-justice agencies.

Evaluation of LEAA

Based on the results of the analysis, how successful is the LEAA? In general, it is having an effect on the ways in which states use federal funds in the criminal-justice area and, therefore, on public policy directed at controlling crime. These effects, however, are clearly only occurring at the margins. This marginal success is to be expected for two reasons: the difficulties involved in altering the policies of systems of organizations enmeshed in state political systems, and the failure of LEAA to effectively coordinate exchange and power-dependence strategies.

Interestingly, LEAA's limited success in reaching its goals is primarily the result of increasing the professionalism of the personnel in SPAs and state and local functional agencies. This exchange strategy has been far more successful in achieving LEAA's goals than the power-dependence strategy of varying the flow of federal funds into states. Insofar as functional allocations have been brought into rough equality and coordination between functional areas has increased as a result of LEAA's efforts, it has been accomplished by staffing SPAs with criminal-justice professionals who are likely to share the same values as the professionals at the federal level. Control of the kind of people involved in policymaking offers a limited kind of control over policy output.

Not all professionals, however, are likely to behave in the same manner. Functional professionals tended to pursue state-priority innovations. In contrast, SPA professionals seemed to emphasize national priorities but only when high levels of discretionary dollars were flowing into the state. Thus the development of higher levels of professionalism at the state and local levels does not necessarily mean that these professionals will pursue specific goals established by LEAA.

We failed to find a consistently significant relationship between the level of either fixed or discretionary block-grant funds and the dependent variables, but this does not necessarily mean that a power-dependence strategy cannot work. These findings indicate that in order for a dependence strategy to be successful, there must be a larger amount of federal funds at stake. In all cases, the size of the total block-grant funds, especially the discretionary funds, was minuscule when compared with the size of state and local criminal-justice budgets. In order for true dependence relationships to be established between LEAA and criminal-justice agencies, the amounts of money must be significant relative to the operating budgets of the agencies. Further, the granting party must be ready and able to withhold these funds if the recipient agencies do not live up to the grantor's expectations. Because the amounts are determined on a formula basis in fixed block-grant funds, the latter condition is not met. In the case of discretionary dollars, the amounts involved are quite small. Further, no evidence was found that LEAA was willing to withhold these funds. In neither case, then, does this stick-and-carrot mode of gaining compliance meet the conditions for effectiveness. The inducements offered are too small, and possible punishments are too remote.

The failure of LEAA to establish a successful power-dependence strategy would explain one of the more puzzling results of the research: the failure of organizational strength to be an important explanatory variable. Recall that proposition 1 in chapter 2 predicted that in the absence of an operative power-dependence strategy, organizations have little incentive to mobilize their resources to resist the changes desired by the granting party. Possibly, organizational strength's unimportance in explaining allocations results from the small amounts of money at stake. Quarrels over the distribution of petty cash may be too unimportant to warrant the mobilization of potential organizational clout.

Another condition for the establishment of a successful power-dependence strategy is the granting party's clear specification of|what it wants done with the money it doles out. This condition has not been met by LEAA. Block-grant funds do not come with specific strings attached. Rather, they are allocated for broadly-defined programs. Given LEAA's vague goals and its limited ability to manipulate block-grant funds, it should come as no surprise that these monies are not instrumental in achieving the agency's goals.

There is evidence that, when specific requirements are attached to block-grant funds, they do have a long-term effect on the ways in which states allocate their funds. Increased funds earmarked for corrections, for example, non-incrementally inflated the base of corrections share of block-grant funds. Following this sharp increase in funding, incrementalism returned—but the new equilibrium was premised on a larger share of the budget for the corrections function. Although consistent evidence of a successful power-dependence strategy was not found, evidence was found that under the right conditions such a strategy could be successful. These conditions for the successful establishment of power-dependence relationships, however, are more likely to be met by grants-in-aid programs than by block grants. Block grants are not without effectiveness. A successful exchange strategy is compatible with their characteristics.

While higher level of funding, more careful earmarking, and the willingness to withdraw funds would no doubt result in closer conformity to LEAA goals, such a strategy would not necessarily be desirable. One of the more troubling results of the analysis is the failure of states' needs to be consistently important in explaining any policy outcomes other than commitment to state-priority innovations. Need was important only when functional professionals were also important and when state priorities were involved. The actual need for a policy may be judged by the decision makers closest to local conditions. Although earmarking may be a way of achieving national goals, the strategy is not very flexible and may ignore the conditions existing in a particular state or locality. It may be possible to establish authoritative federal control, but the rationality of such a strategy is a very different question. Despite these problems, in the most recent LEAA reauthorization of December 1979, Congress earmarked 10 percent of all grant monies to be used to fund national-priority projects.[1]

The Future of LEAA

Despite its current status as an embattled agency facing possible elimination, congressional actions in December 1979 continued LEAA for another four years.[2] As a result of this reauthorization, changes have been made in the agency's structure. Responsibility for research and statistical works has been transferred from LEAA to two newly created agencies: the Bureau of Justice Statistics (BJS) and the National Institute of Justice (NIJ). In addition, Congress created the Office of Justice Assistance, Research and Statistics (OJARS) to coordinate the programs of LEAA, BJS, and NIJ. These changes in its tasks and autonomy will undoubtedly have a substantial effect on the operation of LEAA at the federal level. While reorganizing some functions of LEAA, however, Congress left the agency's responsibilities for administering fixed block and discretionary grants intact. Eighty percent of LEAA funds will go to fixed grants, with 10 percent devoted to discretionary grants and the remaining 10 percent going to national priority projects.

This balance of funding indicates that our conclusions are valid, even in light of LEAA's reorganizations. The limited amounts of available discretionary funds militate against successful power-dependence strategies. The findings about commitment to innovations suggest that it is unrealistic to assume that earmarking 10 percent of all LEAA monies to national-priority programs will have a significant or desirable effect on state and local criminal-justice agencies. When dispersed among fifty states, this amount is unlikely to alter the policies of criminal-justice agencies. It will not constitute a sufficiently large proportion of local agencies' budgets to induce their cooperation with federal policymakers. Also, federal-level priorities do not necessarily coincide with the need for a policy in a specific state. LEAA might use its limited funds more profitably in encouraging the further development of professionalization at the state and local level (that is, reinforcing existing exchange relations) and allowing personnel closest to the situation to decide on a mix of appropriate policies.

As an agency under attack, LEAA has become increasingly vulnerable to budget cuts, even complete elimination. In such a situation, it is reasonable to assume that the agency will be facing, at best, a continually shrinking budget. With fewer resources at its disposal, LEAA cannot realistically hope to establish the kind of power-dependence relationships that it failed to establish during times of more abundant resources. The constraints of its situation leave only one route open to effective influence: LEAA must focus almost exclusively on developing its exchange strategy.

Endemic to federal systems of government is the question of the trade off between federal control and sensitivity to local conditions. The costs and benefits of federal, as opposed to state and local control, over public policy have been debated throughout the history of the United States. LEAA is, of course, a product of the vigorous federal-policy initiatives of the late 1960s, initiatives that are currently perceived largely as failures. This perception rekindled the debate over the shape of federalism in the 1970s, and there is no sign that it will be resolved in the 1980s. This work's approach and empirical analyses can be used to shed some light on this debate. How is it possible to design a federal system of government with the proper balance between centralized control and local autonomy?

Interorganizational Theory and the Study of State Politics and Public Policy

While this book has been specifically concerned with the Law Enforcement Assistance Administration, its findings have relevance for the study of comparative state politics and public policy in general.

Contributions to the Study of State Politics

In an advance over most studies of state politics, we conceptualize state agencies as series of interorganizational systems and focus on the strategies employed by the federal government to influence these systems. First, this approach emphasizes the significance of bureaucratic structures on the policymaking process—an often ignored aspect of the political process in the comparative analysis of the American states. Second, by focusing on the federal impact on state agencies, the study of state policymaking is integrated with the general study of federalism. Significantly, this focus avoids a major problem of most conceptualizations of state politics: treating states as closed systems. By focusing on the SPA, we were able to analyze an agency that is influenced both by the configuration of power at the state level and federal policymakers in LEAA. Treating the state as an open system permits the evaluation of the impact of intrastate and extrastate factors and necessitates a consideration of the theoretical literature on the relationship between organizations and environment.

The results of adopting this approach, as reflected in the empirical findings, have been encouraging. One of the most important findings was that the sharing of values by professional policymakers at different levels of government—exchange—was a more important factor in shaping policy than was the manipulation of federal funding—power dependence. This finding was consistent over the three aspects of LEAA policy that were examined. From the perspective of the study of state politics and federalism, these results are interesting because they indicate that the personnel of state agencies measurably affect the policies pursued by these agencies. Further, the degree to which personnel in different agencies share values is an important determinant of the extent to which these agencies will share policy priorities. The results are also particularly important as we enter an age of fiscal austerity. They indicate that it is not necessarily the case that increases in federal funds lead to a greater degree of compliance with federal objectives. Pursuing an exchange strategy may be more effective and far less expensive than the creation of power-dependence relationships.

The public policies of the American states can no longer be understood without considering the influence of policymaking at many levels of government. It is necessary, therefore, to examine states' public policies in the context of federalism and the wider intergovernmental system. Recent developments in the study of interorganizational relations provide a theoretical framework for such an examination.

Contributions to the Study of Public Policy

Our approach is intended as a contribution to the development of more complete models of public policymaking. Three aspects of the approach and findings ought to be of particular interest to students of public policy: the refinement and applications of an interorganizational approach to the study of policymaking, the incorporation of policy need into an analysis of resource allocation, and the analysis of policy innovation.

As noted, current organizational theory focuses on the relationship between an organization and its environment. Almost without exception, however, examinations of the impact of bureaucracy on public policy have failed to consider the impact of the environment of organizations on their structure and outputs. This book is one of the first to incorporate formally environmental factors into the study of the impact of organizations on policymaking. Moreover, it has gone beyond considering the effects of an undifferentiated environment. The focus is on the impact of the organizational characteristics of an agency's environment on its policies. Drawing on the literature on systems of organizations, two alternative strategies for interorganizational influence have been conceptualized: the power-dependence and exchange strategies. Since intergovernmental relations in the United States are aptly characterized as interorganizational relations, this analysis of these strategies should serve to illuminate some previously unexamined aspects of the federal system.

In a second contribution to the analysis of public policy, this research has introduced and employed a measure of need for a policy. Much scholarly debate has considered whether policy is made rationally or incrementally. Minimally, a rational allocation of resources responds to existing needs for those resources. Incrementalism, on the other hand, assumes that resources are simply allocated on the basis of past allocational decisions regardless of extant needs. Because a policy area has been studied in which level of economic development does not determine resource allocation, comparison of the relative explanatory power of rational and incremental models of policymaking has been possible. Surprisingly, although incrementalism was only moderately evident, need failed to emerge as an important determinant of policymaking. Freeing policymaking from the iron grip of incrementalism, then, does not necessarily mean that policymakers will adopt more rational decision-making rules. Pressures toward incremental decisions are not solely responsible for nonrational policymaking. A plethora of pressures in agencies' environments prevents policymakers from emphasizing need as an important guide to decision making.

Finally, this research contributes to the study of innovation in policymaking. We have moved beyond the binary conceptualization of a policy system as either accepting or rejecting an innovation. Instead innovation is treated as an interval variable by measuring commitment to innovation. Such a measure separates adoptions that are backed by an adequate commitment of resources from adoptions that are only cosmetic measures.[3] This conceptualization provides a better indication of innovativeness than do prior conceptualizations of adoption-nonadoption.

The analysis of innovation yielded several interesting findings. Commitment to state-priority innovations, for example, was highest where local functional agencies were staffed by professionals: only in this situation was policy need an important factor in committing resources to innovations. This finding would not have been made with a more traditional adoption-nonadoption measure of innovation.

The results of this study indicate that theories of interorganizational relations need to be carefully incorporated into studies of policymaking. As modern societies grow more organizationally dense, it will become increasingly difficult to explain public policies without examining their interorganizational determinants.

Public Policymaking in Federal Systems

This book began by discussing the problems that confront federal systems in making and administering public policies. As these nations become more complex, the problems of coordinating the movements of the many autonomous actors in such systems increase drastically. In many ways this book has been an attempt to confront theoretically the problem of steering federal systems. It has been argued that the best way to understand the problem is to conceptualize such political systems as a series of interorganizational systems. The burgeoning literature on interorganizational relations was used to provide an understanding of the dynamics of change in federal systems.

Our work implies that the prospects for centrally directing public policies are constrained by the resistance to change in systems of organizations. The literature on interorganizational relations suggest that such change is best pursued through exchange and power-dependence strategies. If there is to be coordination among these systems of organizations, it must be achieved either through creating relationships of dependence between the federal and other levels of government or through the creation of a set of values shared by policymakers at all levels of the system.

One of the few points of agreement among organizational theorists is the difficulty of changing the structures or outputs of organizations.[4] Further, recent attempts to examine the importance of an organization's environment and its relations with other organizations also conclude that organizations tend to seek autonomy and resist becoming dependent on actors in their environment. These findings all underscore the difficulties involved in attempts to coordinate the policies pursued by fairly autonomous systems or organizations at various levels of government.

At two critical points in the policy process, it is crucial that federal policymakers not underestimate these considerable difficulties: when they evaluate and attempt to understand the success or failure of various types of policies, and when they are drafting new policy. This hitherto ignored literature offers a new understanding of the problems inherent in federal systems. It also offers an explanation of the expenses—in dollars and administrative oversight—involved in such a system. The body of literature stresses the large amounts of money necessary to establish power-dependence relationships and the necessity of careful control through close monitoring. Thus federal-control strategies may be expensive and administratively cumbersome. If nothing else, interorganizational theory gives a sense of the variety of costs involved, whatever the benefits may be, in the establishment by the federal government of uniform policies. This sort of insight is particularly relevant during a period of budgetary retrenchment at all levels of government. If the federal government is going to spend less rationally, the effect of cutbacks on federal control over policy outcomes must be understood.

The research presented and the approach adopted in this book are particularly timely. Scholars of all political persuasions are interested in reconsidering the proper balance of power between federal, state and local governments, as well as the optimal policymaking structures at each of these levels. The perceived failures of the massive federal programs of the 1960s led to a reevaluation of what the federal government could and should do to guide and coordinate the political system.[5]

Scholars are now engaged in a lively debate over the best way to structure a policymaking system that meets criteria of equity, efficiency, and effectiveness while simultaneously remaining responsive to citizen demands. The two opposing positions in this debate mirror the two alternative models of policymaking elaborated by Aaron Wildavsky: intellectual cogitation and social interaction.[6] *Intellectual cogitation* involves, wherever feasible, the setting of a single uniform policy by a central authority. The policy is judged to be the correct alternative and is enforced throughout the political system. This alternative is selected via something approaching an ideal-type model of rational decision making. Enforcement and implementation of policies made through intellectual cogitation presumably involve the use of large centralized bureaucracies at all levels.

In contrast, *social interaction* is a market-oriented method of policymaking. According to this model, policy decisions are made, to the greatest extent possible, by actors pursuing their own interests in either small jurisdictions or through direct forms of democracy. Individuals are assumed to be best able to maximize their own self-interest. In such a system there is no single policy in any issue area. Each state or locality decides on its own mix of public policies with minimal interference by the federal government.

Both of these models have their proponents in the literature on federalism. Sundquist and Davis implicitly defend the intellectual cogitation model.[7] They argue that the federal government must take increasing responsibility for coordinating and overseeing public policy in the United States. They advocate the creation of regional bodies that would serve as the federal coordinators of the states in the regions. Each state would be judged according to its abilities and would be given various degrees of autonomy depending on the judgment made by the federal government. As Wildavsky points out, this system would involve increasing centralization and reducing state and local policymaking autonomy.[8] Sundquist's and Davis's goal is a uniform set of public policies, arrived at through intellectual cogitation, enforced throughout the country.

At the other end of the spectrum from the Sundquist-and-Davis position is the *public-choice* perspective of Vincent Ostrom.[9] He advocates a more decentralized and market-oriented federal system. Such a system would include a good deal more state and local autonomy than is currently the case. National policy would then emerge through what Wildavsky calls social interaction. Each state and locality would decide on the mix of policies most appropriate for it, and there would be no uniform national policy. Finally, localities would be free to contract out to private producers. Government would no longer be a monopoly supplier of public goods and services.

The approach developed here and the findings obtained have important implications for this debate. Most important, the interorganizational approach highlights the problems involved with designing a system involving increased centralized federal control. Such control can either be established through power-dependence or exchange strategies. In the current governmental fiscal crisis, however, it is highly unlikely that the federal government will spend the amounts of money necessary for the creation of power-dependence relationships in a wide variety of policy areas.

Eliminating the power-dependence strategy means that an exchange strategy must be employed to create the tightly coupled federal system envisioned by Sundquist and Davis. This strategy would require an extremely high level of shared values by policymakers at all levels of the system. Such an outcome is difficult to engineer, however, and once produced does not always guarantee agreement on the "proper" (as defined by federal policymakers) course of action. As was found, the use of a pure exchange strategy, as in the case of commitment to innovation, may not lead state and local professionals to pursue specific federal-policy objectives. Only when there was evidence of an operative power-dependence strategy, along with the high SPA professionalism required by the exchange strategy, was there an emphasis on national priorities. For these reasons, the Sundquist-and-Davis approach would require a high degree of reliance on power-dependence strategies.

The analysis in this book, however, has highlighted the problems involved in relying on a power-dependence strategy. The major problem is the large amounts of money that would have to be involved. In the analysis of LEAA, in order for dependence relationships to be established, the amounts involved must be a higher percentage of state-agency budgets than the maximum of 5 percent involved in LEAA block grants: the amount must constitute a significant proportion of the agencies' resources. Further, even if these dependence relationships are established, the resultant policies may not be well tailored to the needs of the areas within which they are implemented. Need failed to be an important explanatory variable except where functional professionals were determining priorities.

The findings underscore the problems that are involved in increasing federal control over specific policies. They also indicate, however, that there is a promising middle road between the opposite strategies suggested by the parties to the debate over designing federal systems. Exchange seemed to be a more efficacious method than power dependence for influencing state and local criminal-justice agencies. Given this general finding, it may be effective to loosen federal controls over the way funds are spent (that is, not attempt to establish power-dependence relationships through expanded grants-in-aid programs, for example), while simultaneously providing incentives for the increased development of professionalized personnel at the state and local level. Once developed, such personnel might be expected to be responsive to the general policy directives of like-minded professionals at the federal level. The careful cultivation of exchange relationships between levels of government would allow overall guidance by federal-level policymakers while simultaneously permitting local determination of specific policies.

It is important to emphasize that we are not advocating professional control of policymaking. In a democratic society, professional values must be augmented by and, in the last instance, subordinated to the decisions reached by representative political structures. Once such decisions have been reached, however, the federal system poses the problem of coordinating policies between levels of government. Our research on coordination suggests that it is achieved more effectively through the creation of shared professional values than by manipulation of large sums of money.

This policy prescription recognizes the prohibitive expense of the sort of tightly coupled–federal system envisioned by Sundquist and Davis, but tries to retain some of its advantages by concentrating on the establishment of successful exchange relations between levels of government. By reducing federal control over the specific use of federal funds, it avoids the problems associated with the possible inappropriateness of centrally designed policies while retaining the influence of federal-level policymakers. In *Speaking Truth to Power,* Wildavsky advocates the design of policy systems that emphasize social interaction, but are guided by intellectual cogitation.[10] A federal system that relied on exchange relationships, based on shared professional values, might result in just the sort of policymaking advocated by Wildavsky.

Wildavsky's suggestions and our findings are particularly relevant to emerging national concerns. Rightly or wrongly, it has become commonplace to blame excessive government spending for the deterioration of the American economy. Consequently, we likely face a period of decline in federal domestic spending. If this situation continues, fewer and fewer relationships of dependence are likely to be established between the federal and other levels of government. In order for federal policymakers to retain some degree of control and influence over state and local decision makers, more attention must be paid to ways of establishing exchange relationships between levels of government. As federal spending is reduced, such a strategy is the only one available to federal policymakers.

The debate over the correct way to structure policymaking in the federal system shows no sign of abating. Analyzing the focus of this debate as a problem in the structuring of interorganizational relations, however, has much promise. We have tried to show that this approach, when applied to LEAA, allows us to analyze not only where the agency succeeds and fails, but why it succeeds and fails. Careful attention, by practitioners and scholars alike, to the insights offered by this interorganizational approach will allow us to move beyond the abstract notions of centralization and decentralization. In their place we suggest a perspective on political systems that stresses the necessity of mixing elements of coercion and persuasion, of federal influence and local autonomy, within the same system. In this manner, we may move toward a pragmatic approach to resolve the problems of federalism—one that maximizes its advantages as a system of democratic government.

Notes

1. *Congressional Quarterly Weekly Reports,* 22 December 1979, pp. 2899-2900.

2. Ibid.

3. George W. Downs, Jr., and Lawrence B. Mohr, "Toward a Theory of Innovation," Institute of Public Policy Studies Discussion Paper no. 92 (February 1977).

4. Michael Hannan and John H. Freeman, "The Population Ecology of Organizations," in *Environments and Organizations,* ed. Marshall W. Mayer (San Francisco: Jossey-Bass, 1978), pp. 131-171.

5. See, for example: Aaron Wildavsky, *Speaking Truth to Power* (Boston: Little, Brown and Co., 1979), part 1.

6. Ibid., ch. 5.

7. James L. Sundquist and David W. Davis, *Making Federalism Work* (Washington, D.C.: Brookings Institution, 1969), pp. 240-250.

8. Wildavsky, 1979, pp. 145-46.

9. Vincent Ostrom, *The Intellectual Crisis in American Public Administration* (University, Ala.: University of Alabama Press, 1973), part 5.

10. Wildavsky, 1979, ch. 5.

Appendix:
Data Sources

Functional Allocations by SPAs

1969

Totals for each state by function were calculated by the authors from a complete listing of projects in U.S., Law Enforcement Assistance Administration, *Annual Report of the Law Enforcement Assistance Administration, 1969* (Washington, D.C.: Government Printing Office, 1969), pp. 9–16.

1970

From 1970 to 1975 the data are taken directly from tables in the annual reports: U.S., Law Enforcement Assistance Administration, *Second Annual Report of the Law Enforcement Assistance Administration, Fiscal Year 1970* (Washington, D.C.: Government Printing Office, 1970), pp. 130–131.

1971

U.S., Law Enforcement Assistance Administration, *Third Annual Report of the Law Enforcement Assistance Administration, Fiscal Year 1971* (Washington, D.C.: Government Printing Office, 1971), pp. 267–268.

1972

U.S., Law Enforcement Assistance Administration, *Fourth Annual Report of the Law Enforcement Assistance Administration, Fiscal Year 1972* (Washington, D.C.: Government Printing Office, 1973), pp. 55–56.

1973

U.S., Law Enforcement Assistance Administration, *LEAA 1973* (Washington, D.C.: Government Printing Office, 1974), pp. 134–135. New categories were used which are different from the format of previous years.

1974

U.S., Law Enforcement Assistance Administration, *Sixth Annual Report of the Law Enforcement Assistance Administration, Fiscal Year 1974* (Washington, D.C.: Government Printing Office, 1975), pp. 209–210.

1975

U.S., Law Enforcement Assistance Administration, *Seventh Annual Report of the Law Enforcement Assistance Administration, Fiscal Year 1975* (Washington, D.C.: Government Printing Office, 1976), pp. 148–149.

1976

A breakdown of block-grant funds by function is not given in the annual report. LEAA provided us with this information for 1976 and 1977 from its computerized data base, the PROFILE system. The 1977 data were not used because it appeared that it was too early in the fiscal year for full reporting by states. The categories provided to us are again different from the format of previous years but since in each year we aggregate several narrow categories into broad categories for the three functions, we do not believe the results are materially different due to format changes.

Extensive discussion with LEAA officials in order to obtain this information did cast some doubt on the accuracy of LEAA's data. For example, a particular project is assigned a functional code by a person at the state level. These coders are not trained so it is possible, though not likely, that what is regarded as a police project in one state is regarded as a corrections project in another state. Also the reporting is less than 100 percent and we do not know if underreporting results in systematic error. The reporting rate has improved over time, however.

Any problems should "wash out" at the highly aggregated level with which we are working. We ran numerous checks on the data, reading project descriptions and doing hand coding, and could not find any systematic error in the data used. If the agency-provided data do not put LEAA in a good light, no other data set will either.

Discretionary Funds, Part C and Part E, Per Capita

1969 to 1972

U.S., Law Enforcement Assistance Administration, *Sixth Annual Report of the Law Enforcement Assistance Administration, Fiscal Year 1974* (Washington, D.C.: Government Printing Office, 1974), pp. 214, 215.

1973 to 1976

U.S., Law Enforcement Assistance Administration, *Eighth Annual Report of the Law Enforcement Assistance Administration, Fiscal Year 1976* (Washington, D.C.: Government Printing Office, 1977), pp. 91, 96. These data are considered to be very good because the records are kept centrally and do not depend on state reporting.

Population, 1970

U.S., Department of Commerce, Bureau of the Census, *Statistical Abstract of the United States, 1972* (Washington, D.C.: Government Printing Office, 1972), p. 12.

Innovations

1969 to 1971

For organized-crime and community-relations projects funded by SPAs, the project titles and program categories listed in annual reports were sufficiently narrow that action grants could be hand coded into these two programs. A complete list of LEAA-funded discretionary projects and recipients was given. They were hand coded into these two categories. U.S., Law Enforcement Assistance Administration, *Annual Report of the Law Enforcement Assistance Administration, 1969* (Washington, D.C.: Government Printing Office, 1969), pp. 9-18; U.S., Law Enforcement Assistance Administration, *Second Annual Report of the Law Enforcement Assistance Administration, Fiscal Year 1970* (Washington, D.C.: Government Printing Office, 1970), pp. 131, 133-201; U.S., Law Enforcement Assistance Administration, *Third Annual Report of the Law Enforcement Assistance Administration, Fiscal Year 1971* (Washington, D.C.: Government Printing Office, 1971), pp. 267, 269-377.

1972 to 1976

A computer search of the PROFILE system was done using appropriate keywords that we supplied. Then we read the project descriptions of the action grants and further narrowed down the list. The list of discretionary grants under each program was produced in the same fashion. We believe these data to be reliable, suffering only from state underreporting.

Joint Projects, 1973 and 1976

We again used the PROFILE system to select all action grants that were classified under more than one function. These data suffer from the same possible biases as the functional allocation data because untrained coders may have classified similar projects differently. Since we checked the computer listings carefully, we have eliminated any false data or overreporting, but we can do nothing about underreporting, that is, the failure to mention that a project affects more than one function. The most reasonable hypothesis is that reporting reliability might vary by state so we compared the state with the highest level of joint activity to the state with the lowest level of activity and found no difference in the types of projects that were classified as joint. Therefore, we believe that these data are a useful measure of joint-functional activity, though probably they are less reliable than the functional allocations and innovations data.

SPA Professionalism, 1976

Information on degrees and current salary of key personnel were obtained from each of the fifty State Planning Applications, 1977, documents that were submitted to LEAA in 1976 and housed in their library thereafter. Key personnel was defined as director; assistant director(s); planning, research, and evaluation directors; heads of police, juvenile, corrections, and courts sections. We used 1976 because it is the only year this information was required. Where this information was missing (which was not often) 1975 data were used and inflated by 5 percent or 1977 data were used and deflated by 5 percent. If the information was still unavailable, written inquiries were directed to the director of the SPA and follow-up efforts were made. There were still a few refusals such as the director who said that federal privacy law prohibits disclosing his employees' salaries when, in fact, federal regulations require him to disclose them.

The amount of SPA budget devoted to libraries and subscriptions was also obtained from the same documents. We believe these data to be very reliable. Unfortunately we cannot reconstruct similar data from earlier years because the documents from earlier years are stored in warehouses. It is unlikely that states reported this information anyway.

Functional Professionalism, 1976

The state and local payroll for each function was divided by the number of full-time equivalent employees at the state and local level in each function to yield an average salary per function in each state. Then these three measures were manipulated in different ways to yield two indices of professionalism. U.S., Law Enforcement Assistance Administration, *Expenditure and Employment Data for the Criminal Justice System, 1976* (Washington, D.C.: Government Printing Office, 1978), pp. 50–56, 59–64.

Organizational Strength, 1976

Each function's proportion of state and local criminal-justice expenditures and proportion of employees were combined to form an index. U.S., Law Enforcement Assistance Administration, *Expenditure and Employment Data for the Criminal Justice System, 1976* (Washington, D.C.: Government Printing Office, 1978), pp. 30–37, 50–56.

Block-Grant Funds, 1976

One measure of dependence is each function's block-grant funds divided by each function's state and local expenditures for 1976. The block-grant funds are a sum of SPA allocations to each function. The expenditure data are from U.S., Law Enforcement Assistance Administration, *Expenditure and Employment Data for the Criminal Justice System, 1976* (Washington, D.C.: Government Printing Office, 1978), pp. 30–37.

Need

Violent-crime rate per 100,000, 1976: The violent-crime rate consists of murder, forcible rape, robbery, and aggravated assault and is somewhat more reliable than is the total-crime index. U.S., Department of Justice, Bureau of Investigation, *Uniform Crime Reports for the United States* (Washington, D.C.: Government Printing Office, 1977), pp. 38–42.

Index

Index

About the Authors

Virginia Gray is an associate professor of political science at the University of Minnesota. Her other professional positions include teaching at the University of Kentucky, serving as a consultant to the Governor's Commission on Crime Prevention and Control (Minnesota), and being a guest scholar at The Brookings Institution. She has published articles in several scholarly journals and has coedited two books on public policy.

Bruce Williams received the Ph.D. from the University of Minnesota and is an assistant professor of political science at The Pennsylvania State University. His articles have appeared in *Law and Public Policy Quarterly* and *Policy Studies Journal.*

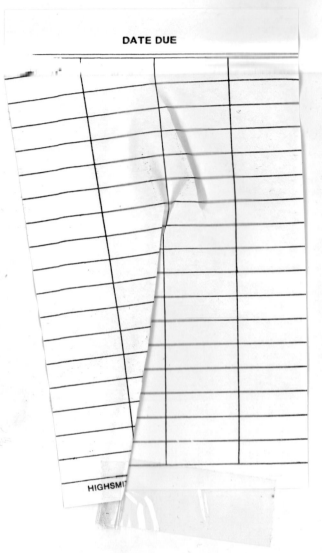

DATE DUE

HIGHSMIT